The Executive Wisdom Management Resources Guide

Consulting | Training| Coaching

GLOBAL LEARNING FOR A GLOBAL AUDIENCE

RIC WILLMOT

Copyright © Ric Willmot 2017

All rights reserved, including the right of reproduction in whole or in part in any form.

This publication contains the opinions and ideas of its author and is designed to provide useful advice and formats to the reader on the subject matter covered. Any references to products or services in that pursuit do not constitute or imply an endorsement or recommendation. The publisher and author specifically disclaim any responsibility for any liability, loss, or risk (financial, personal, or otherwise) which may be claimed or incurred as a consequence, directly or indirectly, of the use and/or application of any of the contents of this publication.

The publisher does not attest to the validity, accuracy, or completeness of this information. Use of a term in this book should not be regarded as affecting validity of any trademark or service mark.

Without limiting the rights under the copyright reserved above, no part of this publication may be reproduced, stored in or introduced into a retrieval system, or transmitted, in any form, or by any means (electronic, mechanical, photocopying, recording, or otherwise), without the prior written permission of Ric Willmot.

For general information about Ric Willmot's products, speaking, and consulting services please call +61 7 3395-1050. Our fax number is +61 7 3395-1805, and our e-mail is info@executivewisdom.com. There are over 300 free, indexed articles to download at http://executivewisdom.com. You may also subscribe at that site to our free, electronic monthly newsletter: The Executive Wisdom Times and the free, electronic weekly snippet: Willmot's Weekly Wisdom.

Please contact us if you are interested in joining the Society for Executive Wisdom an organisation dedicated to improving the business and influence of Owners, CEOs, Executives and Managers.

Copyright © 2017 Ric Willmot

All rights reserved.

ISBN: 1979193487

ISBN-13: 978-1979193481

RW
Ric Willmot

Tools and Resources by Ric Willmot

Books

- Professional Services Marketing Wisdom: How to attract, influence and retain clients even if you hate selling
- Writing in Business for Success & Profits: The Professionals Desktop Companion
- Change 601: How to Create Successful Long-Lived Organisational Change
- Change Management 601: Pragmatic Solutions for Change Management Problems
- Ric's Rants Willmot's Wisdom
- Exploding the Leadership Myth
- Successful Business Writing Templates: Every Business Letter, Memo and Inquiry You Require In A Thriving Professional Services Firm

Booklets

- Brainstorming Your Business to Sales Success
- How to Improve Your Business

E-Books

- Fundamental Value Proposition Workbook
- The Referral Handbook

Audio CDs

- Expanding Existing Business (Teleconference Recording)
- Get ready for and triumph over Objections (Teleconference Recording)
- Getting to the Buyer (Teleconference Recording)
- Identify Your Existing and Potential Prospects (Teleconference Recording)
- Law Firm Marketing Masters Interview
- Networking Smart for Results (Teleconference Recording)
- Secrets of Time Management (Teleconference Recording)
- The Business Leader's Toolkit
- Value Based Pricing (Teleconference Recording)

Learning Modules

- Psychology of Critical Decision-Making
- Change Management 601: And why there is no Change Management 101
- Strategic Planning Toolkit (Manual & Data CD)
- Strategic Thinking Learning Module

Newsletters

- The Executive Wisdom Times Monthly Newsletter ISSN 2201-5973
- Willmot's Weekly Wisdom ISSN 1837-8552
- The Private Client's Mentor Program Newsletter

The Executive Wisdom Management Resources Guide

Consulting | Training | Coaching

GLOBAL LEARNING FOR A GLOBAL AUDIENCE

RIC WILLMOT

CONTENTS

- WHY INVEST IN LEARNING & DEVELOPMENT? 1
- TESTIMONIALS 4
- EXECUTIVE WISDOM ACTION LEARNING 6
- LEARNING & DEVELOPMENT CHECKLIST 10
- EXECUTIVE WISDOM IN-HOUSE TRAINING COURSES 13
- *Leadership Power:* MASTERING LEADERSHIP FOR A MORE EFFECTIVE & DYNAMIC ORGANISATION 18
- *Transformational Leadership:* HOW LEADERS CAN EFFECT SUCCESSFUL CHANGE IN COMPANIES, ORGANISATIONS, AND TEAMS 20
- *Strategic Thinking Skills:* UNRAVELLING CHAOS AND HARNESSING THE POWER OF YOUR ORGANISATION TO IMPROVE RESULTS 22
- *Strategy Unwrapped:* STRATEGIC THINKING, PLANNING, & IMPLEMENTATION IN A VOLATILE MARKET 24
- *Art Of Conflict Management:* HOW TO EFFECT SUCCESSFUL RESOLUTIONS IN COMPANIES, ORGANISATIONS, AND TEAMS 26
- *Leading Organisational Change & Transformation:* HOW TO TRANSFORM YOUR ORGANISATION TO SURVIVE AND PROSPER IN AN AGE OF DISRUPTION 28
- *Critical Decision Making:* HOW TO EFFECT BETTER, SUCCESSFUL DECISIONS IN COMPANIES, ORGANISATIONS, AND TEAMS 30
- *4-Day Program: Senior Management Transformation:* MANAGING ORGANISATIONAL CHANGE, BUSINESS TRANSFORMATION, STAKEHOLDER ENGAGEMENT, AND COMMUNICATIONS 32
- *Business Negotiations Skills:* THE ART & SCIENCE OF NEGOTIATING THE BEST DEAL 36
- *Effective Communication Skills:* EFFECTIVE BUSINESS COMMUNICATION EQUALS GREATER ORGANISATIONAL SUCCESS 38
- *Master Class: Critical Business Skills For Success:* LEARNING THE BUSINESS EXECUTION TECHNIQUES OF STARS LIKE: AMAZON, APPLE, NIKE & STARBUCKS 40
- *Argumentation:* A GUIDE TO EFFECTIVE REASONING AND ITS ROLE IN ORGANISATIONS AND MANAGEMENT 44
- *Creative Thinking Skills:* THE CREATIVE THINKER'S TOOLKIT FOR TRANSFORMATIVE LEADERS & MANAGERS 46
- *Critical Thinking Skills:* A SCIENTIFIC GUIDE TO CRITICAL THINKING AND THE ROLE OF YOUR DECEPTIVE MIND 48
- *Building Brain Fitness:* HOW TO OPTIMISE YOUR BRAIN'S POWER 50
- *Psychology Of Influence:* CREATING A HIGH PERFORMANCE ORGANISATION 52
- *Scepticism As A Business Tool:* HOW MANAGEMENT CAN THINK LIKE A SCIENTIST 54
- *The Hidden Factor:* THINKING DIFFERENTLY TO ACHIEVE ORGANISATIONAL SUCCESS 56

Marketing Wisdom: HOW TO ATTRACT, INFLUENCE AND RETAIN CLIENTS EVEN IF YOU HATE SELLING 58

Guerrilla Marketing Bootcamp: TURBOCHARGE YOUR MARKETING PERFORMANCE 60

Design Your Own Programs: GENERATING RAPID RESULTS WITH SHORT COURSES 66

CONSULTING 74

TYPICAL CLIENT RESULTS 81

MENTORING & COACHING 87

PROFESSIONAL SPEAKING 97

BONUS MATERIALS 99

ENGAGE RIC WILLMOT TO BE A MEMBER OF YOUR BOARD 111

SOME OF OUR CLIENTS 113

ABOUT RIC WILLMOT 115

HOW TO ENGAGE RIC WILLMOT & EXECUTIVE WISDOM 117

WHY INVEST IN LEARNING & DEVELOPMENT?

If you wish to increase the standards, performance, and results of any group, improving the top of the pile is not nearly as effective as concentrating your effort on the foundation or base instead. Simple example: Getting a Toyota hybrid electric vehicle to reduce from 4.5L/100km to 3.5L/100km isn't nearly as valuable and important as getting a Ford SUV to trim down from 7.5L/100km to 6.5L/100km. There are two reasons for this. The first is that there are a lot more Ford SUVs than Toyota hybrids. The second is that Ford SUVs use many more litres of petrol, so a percentage increase has far more yield. (You cannot average averages).

If you care about health and a culture of performance, it's tempting to push Olympic athletes, to go a tenth of a second faster. It's much more worthwhile and effective, though, if you can get 3,000,000 children to each spend five additional minutes every day walking instead of sitting.

Organisations pamper and challenge the few in the executive suite, imagining that one more good decision in the business development team could pay off. The thing is, if every one of the 10,000 customer-facing employees was more engaged, helpful and kind, it would have a far more significant impact on the company and those it serves. I believe the reason we focus on the few, is that it feels more dramatic, seems more controllable and is ultimately easier. However, the useful, fair and important thing to do is to help the back of the line catch up.

Employee retention is a huge challenge (and expense) for employers. So is the hiring process. Having a robust employee development program can help make that less of a burden. When it comes to attracting and hiring the best employees, here's why a solid employee development program matters:

- *It is a benefit.* Staff learning and development can be seen as a benefit, and that is something employees weigh in the *pros column* when finding a job. Providing employee development as part of the hiring package gives you a competitive advantage over other similar jobs and wages.

- *It builds loyalty.* Loyal employees aren't prone to quitting. That's what employee retention is all about. Knowing that an employer is willing to provide training and development makes an employee feel important, and it makes them loyal.

- *It increases your reputation.* Having a reputation as a good employer — one who cares enough to provide training — is tremendous both for hiring new employees as well as how customers see your organisation. Word gets out about who is fabulous to work for, and that can affect sales as well as the hiring process.

- *It brings in the best people.* By offering training, continuing education, conference attendance, or even something as simple as a book allowance, with the understanding that you expect them to participate, you will attract employees who are looking to improve themselves. That's an employee you want to hire.

Promoting managers and other upper-level employees from within your organisation is worthwhile. Who else is more familiar with your day-to-day business, stakeholders, and customers? But not every long-time employee is ready for such positions and promoting them when they are not prepared leads to problems. A proper employee development program will:

- Create a pool of capable workers.
- Create workers ready for promotion.
- Help you identify strengths and weaknesses in your employees.

Employee development trains your current people for possible future promotion as well as identifying those employees who have the aptitude for such a promotion. Better to learn about strengths and weaknesses in training rather than when the pressure is mounting and success is crucial.

Learning and development also keeps employees engaged at work. Bored employees are a recipe for disaster. They easily take on negative attitudes, sloppy work habits, and cause damage to relationships with other employees, stakeholders, and customers. Employee development is a way that you can keep your employees engaged at work to prevent that kind of boredom from setting in. Exciting and valuable training programs, and future development events that are fun or challenging to look forward to — removes the drudgery of a job that may lead to that dreaded boredom.

Furthermore, a good employee is like money in the bank. Well-trained, confident, and engaged employees will perform better in the long run. That's going to help save you money, as employees become more efficient and proficient. Employee development also has the potential to increase sales and output. Either way, that's good for your bottom line, and that's why Sarvadi classified employee development not as an expense, but as an investment.

Employee development is a continual process, and that means you always must be planning for the future. You'll be asking yourself:

- What kind of leadership will I need?
- What will my customers need from my employees?
- What industry changes might I expect?

Since your employees are integral to any answer arrive at, their training and development are tightly involved, as well. That's what forces you to think ahead because employee development programs don't happen without planning. The training that worked last year might not work next year. Your business culture may be changing according to your customer and industry needs. You might need to attract a different type of employee, and your development offerings need to adapt and reflect that.

An employee development plan that's going to work necessarily forces you to consider the future path of your business. That's a positive thing. Staying on your toes regarding relevant employee development means you'll be thinking ahead of the curve for your organisation.

Executive Wisdom is globally recognised as providing cutting-edge consulting, coaching, and learning and development for executive management, leaders, board members, and owners. Additionally, Executive Wisdom delivers world-class learning and coaching to frontline staff and managers because we have always known that improved organisational performance requires increased competency and capacity of the entire personnel, not just a select few.

This is why we have created this resource for organisations like yours. I trust that you gain value from the book and it helps you plan your learning and development to dramatically improve results.

Ric Willmot

TESTIMONIALS

"Ric is a terrific advocate of challenging conventions and can provide thought provoking insight to any business. I recommend him to any organisation that wants a truly candid assessment of their strategy or operations and is looking for ways to improve."
Sean Rennick — QLD Manager, Telstra

"A total of 139 attendees responded to the evaluation process on your presentation at our recent conference and your overall rating was 4.8 out of 5!"
Samantha French — National Events Manager, CPA Australia

"Thank you once again for your valuable contribution to our planning session. My State Manager said it was 'the best planning retreat we've ever had' and your contribution was essential to that outcome."
Shane Campbell — Deputy State Manager, AusIndustry

"Thank you again! We intend to keep working with you Ric. With your experience, knowledge, intellectual grunt and honest and direct style – we know we are in good hands."
Tess Sanders Lazarus — Managing Director, Invigorate

"I was fortunate to use the services of Ric here at New Hope Coal. Ric was an invaluable participant in this project as his objective and persuasive argument challenged the thinking of our managers. I was also fortunate to witness Ric's mastery in quickly developing rapport with each of our managers, which is not something I have seen from many other consultants. In addition, while it was not part of his brief, Ric assisted me on a personal development level to understand how to deal with some difficult situations that I face from time to time."
Dianne Armbrust — HR Director, New Hope Coal

"From the outset Ric developed rapport with everyone in the room, his unique ability of working with his audience, and to have each and every one focused on the topic at hand is rarely seen or experienced. Ric's knowledge and his innovative approach had everyone's attention for the entire day. I gained a clear insight into taking my business to a new level, by developing new strategies."
Helen Pass — Owner, Corporate Concierge

"Ric's presentation 'How to Wake up the Leadership Genius Inside You' gave me excellent insights into motivating staff and getting buy-in. I learned a lot about my own leadership style. I recommend Ric to anyone who is looking to develop their leadership skills."
Brendan O'Keefe — QLD Manager, Translink

"All I can say is that you were brilliant!"
Kerrie Algeo — Executive Officer, Beaudesert Shire Council

"Ric has a unique ability in working with people to help them identify and understand their own character and others to enable them to form better working relationships. Ric has the Midas touch in bringing out the potential in all."
Nick McGuire — Executive Officer, Scenic Rim Regional Council

"Thank you Ric, strategic planning took on a whole new meaning. This whole exercise showed how we can achieve fantastic results."
Rhonda Brown — Principal, Gravity Central

"Dear Ric, I am writing to convey my profound gratitude to you for providing me with the most inspirational and educational days of my life. Although you shared a huge amount of information with us in a relatively short time, you were first class and made absorbing this powerful information extremely easy and so much FUN. It was of enormous value that I will be receiving for the rest of my life as I put what I have learned into practice. Thank you seems so inadequate. To anyone who's considering whether to avail themselves of any of your services I say ... Do it! You'll never regret it."
Vicki Lennox — Managing Director, Emerging Swan

"In a growing market like Dubai where trends and competition are on a high level, Ric's 'Leadership Innovation Formula' brought creative ideas to engage and enthuse the audience of over 60 senior public and private sector leaders. Ric's cutting-edge thinking added to the successful delivery. ERAM, Tanmia and Motorola were pleased to have Ric conduct this program in Dubai!"
Rima Khodr — Managing Director, ERAM International

"Ric has a very heart warming and engaging style that captured the audience attention from his opening words right through to his closing statement. With a perfect balance of humour, storytelling and anecdotal wisdom he delivered in a manner that went straight to the core of management, innovation and customer service. He has an impeccable understanding of how to relate to his audience, what to give them and how to present it."
Dr. Ricki Jeffrey — CEO, Rockhampton Regional Development Limited

"Ric is a very effective consultant who gets his innovative message across. Any cost associated with getting to hear him is easily offset by the improvement in your business."
Mike O'Hagan — Owner and CEO, MiniMovers

EXECUTIVE WISDOM ACTION LEARNING

Many organisations spend enormous amounts of money and time on training packages and management development of one form or another. Organisations invest in developing their people only because someone believes the organisation will become more productive as a result. However, the question needs to be asked: with what result? Over the last 30 years, there is little or no evidence to suggest the time and money that has been spent on training by organisations has produced any sustained contribution to individual and organisational effectiveness.

There are some simple, yet powerful, principles which underpin successful management education:

- A focus on learning rather than teaching.
- A focus on actionable outcomes.
- A direct relationship of individual competencies to strategic organisational issues.
- Involvement of the participants and clients in the design and running of the program.
- The use of real issues rather than case studies and simulations.
- Keeping participants at work and bringing the learning to the job.
- Promoting competence ahead of qualifications.
- Generating a tangible return on investment.

If you study most management development practiced in Asia, the Middle East, and South Pacific currently, you will see they violate a number of these basic principles for improvement in individual and organisational effectiveness. Executive Wisdom Action Learning (EWAL) is a methodology which aims and strives to adhere to these principles and which does, in my opinion, produce results for the individual and the organisation.

Executive Wisdom Action Learning (EWAL)

Action learning is a term coined by Reg Revans in the 1950s to describe the way in which managers can work on real projects to make significant organisational improvement, while simultaneously enhancing individual skills. Executive Wisdom has tested and implemented action learning throughout numerous organisations in many countries over the last three decades. Surprisingly, action learning is practiced far less by other organisational development consultants and trainers than warranted by its success.

- Everyone taking part in an Executive Wisdom Action Learning (EWAL) program must have a meaningful and significant project.
- This project must be nominated and sponsored by a senior manager or executive in the organisation.
- The senior manager or executive must have the authority to recommend, support, and promote the project.
- The senior manager or executive must be prepared to take a genuine interest in the work and is willing and able to act on the results.

Executive Wisdom Action Learning (EWAL) represents a genuine organisational effort rather than an individual employee pursuing her or his path for personal interest. Action learning is, in my opinion, the only practiced learning approach that will make a critical and joint contribution to organisational and managerial effectiveness, simultaneously. By taking this course of action, an organisation is investing in a methodology that delivers real and tangible efficiency improvements, increasing the uniformity of culture and vision, and more versatile, capable managers, executives, and leaders.

Executive Wisdom Action Learning (EWAL) produces real, measurable, and ordered gains for both the individual and the organisation because it distinguishes learning to produce organisational outputs and results rather than the current form of staff "training and teaching" that is not linked to outcomes.

Executive Wisdom Action Learning — Basic Principles

*Executive Wisdom Action Learning is about real people working together on—
and learning from—real and current problems in a systematic way to improve
both the organisation and themselves.*

- The learning comes directly from real and current organisational problems—the primary vehicles for successful action learning are the issues that the participants have contracted to address. Every other design element is secondary to this core precept.
- Consequently, there is a place for expert external input insofar as it aids participants to gain more learning from dealing directly with their contracted problems or projects in a systematic way.
- The learning comes from people working together, helping each other understand and address their contracted problems or projects. That being so, there are regular forums for participants to meet, develop strong supportive working relationships, and join the Executive Wisdom Coaching Program and Executive Wisdom Online Forum.
- The Executive Wisdom Action Learning (EWAL) process:
  - arises out of actions that participants engage in on a real organisational problem
  - followed by a period of reflection where they identify the learning which has occurred
  - is then generalised into a set of principles for similar or different situations
  - leads participants to apply these learnings to new problems

- The learning is systematic—it involves a guided, structured process which is modelled to the participants in the early stages of an Executive Wisdom Action Learning (EWAL) program, and which they adopt while advancing through the program.

- The problem or issue that a participant brings to the program is real and current. It is the sort of problem that will make a difference to organisational efficiency and effectiveness when resolved.

- Executive Wisdom Action Learning (EWAL) leads to improvement in participants. In particular, it develops managers and leaders who—by their own acclaim and that of their direct superiors—become empowered, confident, more knowledgeable, more skilled, and more resourceful.

- It also leads to improvements in the organisation. I have been involved with more than 64 action learning programs in 49 different organisations in 8 countries over 13 years; every one of them has produced savings at least 4½ times the cost of running the program within six months of its completion. In one case, it produced gains equal to at least 20 times the program cost within two years of its ending. However, this is not all there is to it – this approach to action also generates less obvious, but very real, improvements in work practices, systems, cultures, and structures.

- The Executive Wisdom Action Learning (EWAL) program is a very active, open, and supportive relationship among three groups: the participants, the organisation's senior managers or executives who sponsor the participants, and the Executive Wisdom Action Learning (EWAL) program team.

- There are many more "participants" involved than merely the delegates, i.e., their subordinates, superiors, other stakeholders in their projects, and their loved ones..

Conclusion

Executive Wisdom Action Learning (EWAL) is about developing your organisation in terms of efficiencies, integration, impacts, and coherence. It is also about empowering and developing executives and managers with skills, knowledge, and awareness to increase their effectiveness, their impact, and their flexibility. However, more importantly, it's about doing these things in a way that makes them directly relevant to the organisation and maximises the fit between the Executive Wisdom Action Learning (EWAL) and the concerns, visions, and goals of the senior executives.

It's not about off-the-shelf solutions, quick fixes, or short-term certainties and promises which fail in the cold light of day. The Executive Wisdom Action Learning (EWAL) is about the development of a mutual relationship between the organisation and the Executive Wisdom team.

It's about delivering genuine and real management and organisational results.

> "Within six months, Ric has taken my staff outside of their comfort zone which has led to astonishing results and improved performance. His dynamic personality forces you to think outside the square. Working with Ric has made me realise the importance of having very succinct goals."
>
> - Julie Kerin, Owner of HB Recruitment & Training

Don't hope for rain!

Strategy and culture: two words commonly overused and underdeveloped. **Ric Willmot** writes.

This month I have been fortunate to work in three burgeoning cities showcasing their beautiful waterfronts.

Hobart, right on Salamanca, Cairns along the esplanade looking out over multi-million dollar yachts and Townsville on the Strand, with its glorious views of Magnetic Island.

While visiting Cairns, a college friend invited me to a home-cooked meal with his family. [A special treat for me, for my wife doesn't cook; although she does make nonpareil reservations!]

While enjoying a pre-dinner drink on their apartment's roof-top entertaining area, Gus' three-year-old daughter, Petra, proudly opened her new umbrella for me to review; then pausing to enquire if it might rain. Many corporate strategies are living in the same deleterious hope.

There are two facets to a company accomplishing its business goals: the business strategy, and the organisational culture that supports it.

Culture is in simple terms that collection of beliefs which hold sway over behaviour. Employees' behaviour must be in concert with the performance necessary to yield the anticipated business results. It's as simple as that!

"Values" exercises and "strategic retreats" to conceive statements of vision and mission are of no value unless they demonstrably influence and shape the decisions day after day, taken by management at all levels all through the organisation.

Here are three of Ric's Strategy Salvo's

1. Values should be seen not just heard

The General Manager of a million dollar subsidiary of a multi-national company explained to me that he didn't approve of the vicious behaviour of one of his Sales Managers, infamous for offensively cudgelling sales representatives in open meetings.

"But you do approve, David," I replied, "because your failure to do anything about it shows other's that Geoffrey's behaviour is the way to succeed here. Not only that, but you are developing Mini-Geoffrey's, and losing quality people who don't feel comfortable in this culture."

Geoffrey was terminated from the company within a month, but the clones took over a year to be converted or exited.

2. Values should be memorable

Values and vision must be concise enough to be used as daily templates for decision making and planning.

All businesses make or lose money each day as the result of decisions made by employees.

Lexus had a mission statement that was the equivalent of "Beat Benz." Komatsu, the heavy equipment manufacturer had one that basically said, "Eat Cat" referring to their rival Caterpillar.

You want your employees to have it in their minds every day on the job, or else they won't be using them to guide decisions and take actions to support the firm.

3. The Buck Stops at the Top

Salespeople, warehouse staff, and customer service operators are held accountable for the amount of their sales, the speed and accuracy of deliveries and their satisfaction of the consumer.

As we climb the hierarchical stairs, measures should become more difficult not easier.

Business leaders must be made responsible for the company's future, quality and results. The helmsman may technically steer the ship, but the captain sets the destination. Navigators simply recommend the best course.

The captain is responsible to the ships' owners and to those who sail in it.

Strolling along the boardwalk on the Cairns esplanade, the mud flats were slowly being replaced by the sea, glistening brilliantly in the morning sun.

You get a sense of the opportunity before us; for there is a rising tide, unless we wish to be a victim of the water. ∎

RIC WILLMOT *is known as "The Consultant's Consultant". He is the CEO of Executive Wisdom Group, www.executivewisdom.com; and the founder of the Society for Executive Wisdom, www.executivewisdomsociety.com*

LEARNING & DEVELOPMENT CHECKLIST

Purpose

- What specific management action are we developing?

- What do we hope to learn?

Buy-In

- What specific changes do we need to make as the basis of this learning?

- How will we ensure that the learning gained is not ignored by our people?

Feasibility

- Do we have the right people chosen for this course? That is motivated to learn and improve?

- What other people do we need to involve in this learning, besides the obvious ones?

- How can we avoid disrupting operations while our people are in training?

Reliability

- Who on this program should receive post-training coaching & mentoring?

- Do the characteristics of the people selected for this training match the vision and objectives of our stated purpose?

- Have we confirmed that all attendees will be engaged in implementing the Executive Wisdom Action Learning pedagogy?

Value

- Can we do a targeted rollout of this learning and development course focusing on areas where the payback is highest?

- Have we implemented all the learning components with the highest returns?

- Do we understand which variables are causing which effects

- Have we ensured that those issues are appropriately addressed in the course program?

Breathing life into your 'system'

Organisations are 'living systems' whose participants are willing to help in their functioning, **Ric Willmot** *writes*

We recognise it is possible to bring about successful organisational change. Organisations have changed not only their mission, procedures, performance levels, but have augmented their capability to manage change in general.

In these organisations, individuals are confident, instilled with a sense of purpose and achievement, and willing to deal with change as a constant event.

Yet research shows almost 75 percent of organisational change efforts do not generate the expected outcomes.

The hard work fails to yield the desired results, but rather delivers a torrent of unintentional and negative consequences; requiring leaders to manage the impact of unwanted effects.

Instead of celebrating new efficiencies created by restructuring, the leader faces a burned out and demoralised group of survivors. Instead of escalating share prices after a merger, leaders clamber in an effort to have people working together.

Failures in organisational change are the product of deep confusion of who people are and what's happening inside organisations.

We participate in a world in the midst of unremitting creation, in a universe whose creativity and adaptability are beyond comprehension. There are maybe 100 million species on the planet, each displaying the ability to change, but humans fail at our change projects and indict each other of being incapable of coping with change.

It's widespread to describe organisations as "organic." Presumably, we no longer consider them as a machine, which was the prevailing notion of organisations, people, and the universe for the past 300 years.

However, these processes continue to be essentially mechanistic.

A segment of the system (the system can be anything; an organisation, a community, a business unit) detects an "event". Maybe a memo, a comment, a report. The segment chooses to be disturbed — the system's right. The organisational segment perceives the information and disseminates it hurriedly via its networks. Elsewhere, the information is interpreted and its meaning intensified. The information transforms, distorts from the original, but continually is amassing greater meaning.

It may billow with such significance that the system can no longer cope with the existing chaos. Only then will the organisational system initiate change.

It is coerced, by the significance of the information, to release present beliefs, structures and values, plunging itself into a state of upheaval and disarray.

Now the system is competent to reorganise into a new form of existence. It reorganises around new interpretations and new meaning. And like all living systems, it has changed because it was the only way it saw to preserve itself.

But how do you create such a 'living system', where participants are willing to deal with change as a constant event? Kellnor-Rogers & Wheatley list four principles:

- Participation is not a choice. We must invite people into the process of rethinking and redesigning the organisation. If involved, they will create a future that already has them in it. No further need for the exhausting tasks of "selling" them the change, gaining "buy-in", or scheming inducements that might persuade them into acquiescent behaviours. For fifty years a piece of wisdom in organisational behaviour states: "People support what they create." We could restate this as: "People only support what they create."
- Life always reacts to directives, it never obeys them. No matter how clear or important the message is, it can only elicit reactions, not compliance. Expect reactions as varied as the individuals who hear it. If we offer our work as an invitation to react, this changes our relationships with all stakeholders. It opens us to the partnering relationships that life craves. Even if we insist on obedience, we will never gain it for long, and we only gain it at the cost of what we wanted most, loyalty, intelligence and responsiveness.
- We do not see "reality." We each create our own interpretation of what's real. We see the world through who we are. And a very important paradox becomes evident. We don't have to agree on an interpretation or have identical values to agree on what has to be done. This paradox flies in the face of how we've tried to reach group consensus, but it makes good sense from a living system's perspective. We all need to participate, and when we're offered that opportunity, we then want to work with others.
- To create better health in a living system, connect it to more of itself. When a system is failing, or performing poorly, the solution will be discovered within the system if better connections are created. The value of this practice was quite evident at the beginning of the customer service revolution, when speaking to customers and dealing with the information they offered became a potent method for stimulating organisations to new levels of quality. Quality standards rose dramatically once customers were connected to the system.

We analyse the details, the structures, values, communication channels, vision,

> "Failures in organisational change are the product of deep confusion of who people are and what's happening inside organisations."

standards, and measures. We let experts or leaders design them, and then strategise how to get them accepted by the organisation.

Living systems have all these features, but they originate differently, from within the system. In a machine where there is no intelligence or creative energy, these features are designed outside and then programmed or engineered in.

We feel obligated to act rather than to inquire. But if we don't begin to seriously focus on learning in our organisations, there is no way we can bring them to life. ■

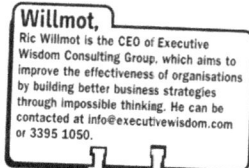

Willmot,
Ric Willmot is the CEO of Executive Wisdom Consulting Group, which aims to improve the effectiveness of organisations by building better business strategies through impossible thinking. He can be contacted at info@executivewisdom.com or 3395 1050.

"We must be doing something right!"

To move up 55 places since 2003 in Queensland's top 400 private companies is quite an achievement.
We must be doing something right by our customers, why not find out more?

ASK US HOW WE CAN HELP YOU TO ACHIEVE GREATER PROFITS AND REDUCE DEBT WRITE-OFFS!

Brisbane
Sydney
Melbourne   **1800 007 886**
Cairns
Adelaide
Perth
Wellington, NZ

DON'T GET DISCONNECTED
...
www.qbr.com.au

EXECUTIVE WISDOM IN-HOUSE TRAINING COURSES

Internal training offers employers and employees advantages that are not found when you send an employee to a public training seminar. In-house training is an effective way to develop your team to optimise performance. Research demonstrates that a key advantage of teams training together is not just around consistency in the knowledge and skills learned (which is a great advantage on its own) but the ongoing interaction around the newly acquired knowledge and skills which guarantees a positive return on investment for both the individual and the organisation long after the training is provided.

Other benefits of In-House training include:

- Cost-effectiveness.
- Customised content aligned to meet your organisation's goals, objectives, policies, procedures, and processes ensuring that the training is relevant to your people and your organisation.
- Improved team performance (*Teams that train together gain together*).
- Demonstrated return on investment (ROI) to the organisation.

Our Executive Wisdom training courses are hands-on and practical where you will be will be exposed to many disparate case studies, group challenges, and individual problem solving exercises that will test your knowledge. We provide a range of quality corporate training solutions from short course formats to five-day programs to twelve-month development training programs. Courses can be supported with:

- Pre-training assessments and diagnostics.
- Pre-training reading materials.
- In-course diagnostics, tools, etc.
- Post-training coaching & mentoring.
- Post-training reviews and assessments.
- Post-training follow-up refresher courses.

Ric Willmot has been delivering public training programs and in-house training programs since 2004. Following are some of the most popular programs delivered by Executive Wisdom, briefly explained by:

- What you will learn.
- Topic Menu.
- How you will stand to benefit as an organisation.
- Who benefits from the course.
- How the course is delivered.
- How many delegates can attend.

We work with you to tailor all training programs to guarantee that your objectives are achieved.

MANAGEMENT RESOURCES GUIDE

Mammoths to Jelly Fish: PNG SME's Need to Prepare for Change

by Ric Willmot

The Russians periodically extract intact from the Siberian ice those ancient woolly mammoths looking akin to a hairy, oversized elephant. These specimens are perfectly preserved in time, much like the business advisors and marketing gurus, which seem perfectly preserved in time somewhere around 1970.

The mammoths, of course, are items of particular scientific and anthropological interest. Business advisors and marketing gurus, unfortunately, we are not so sure about. Why are we still reading about search engine optimisation, 360-degree feedback evaluations, and sales appointment ratios and closing rates?

Google keep changing the rules about SEO. So, stop wasting money on it. Employee evaluations that review past performance are non-sensical and add no future value to an employer. And, analyses of sales appointment ratios and closing rates hardly qualify as an intelligent measurement of marketing activity. Most of the sales and marketing training and workshops that are vaunted today were originally manifest in the 1960s in fields such as insurance, advertising, and the like. Frankly, they just aren't valid today in a more discerning and sceptical business environment.

I once had a business owner complain to me that a saleswoman on his staff—who was producing more business than everyone else in the organisation—wouldn't get out of the office and make sales calls. "She stays at the desk talking on the phone all day. What do you think I should do about her, Ric?"

"Get her a more comfortable chair."

The war for business in the SME arena is fiercer than ever with multitudes of providers offering discounts and incentives. In days of yore, good SMEs were jealously sought-after and preferred by customers over big corporates who only treated customers as numbers. However, as Bob Dylan said, "The times they are a changing."

SMEs are continually making compromises, adjustments and trade-offs on a regular basis. Furthermore, this frequently leads to deficient quality; costing everyone not only money but time, aggravation and repute. SMEs that have a desire to deliver exceptional quality and build long-term, valuable relationships need to submit to rigorous additional learning and invest in more intelligent, respectful marketing and sales processes.

Success will reward the informed and astute SMEs who can engage prospective clients with enthusiasm and respect. Ironically, while lesser quality vendors are doing somersaults to superficially influence and manipulate their customers, SMEs that believe in their value and charge appropriately will be treated with far more consumer-loyalty and win much more business.

SMEs in PNG have an opportunity to stand out from the crowd rather than continuing to blend in with the mosaic. The world is demanding change. People have tired from being lectured to and taken for granted by the elite, media, politicians, and big corporates. Brexit and Donald Trump are the results of mainstream citizens finding their voice again and demanding to be heard. Consumers are the same. Customers want to be heard and are demanding a change in attitude from business.

SMEs by dint of their business models have greater flexibility and can more readily adapt to the changes that consumers demand. This places SMEs ahead of the curve before the big corporates have even recognised the marketplace are deserting them in preference to another. But SMEs in PNG must accept they are competing globally because of the internet. Anybody can buy anything and have it delivered anywhere at any time. The two necessary improvements required are: strategy and culture.

There are two facets to a PNG-SME accomplishing its business goals: the business strategy, and the organisational culture that supports it. Culture is in simple terms that collection of beliefs which hold sway over behaviour. Employees' behaviour must be in concert with the performance necessary to yield the anticipated business results. It's as simple as that.

"Values" exercises and "strategic retreats" to conceive statements of vision and mission are of no value unless they demonstrably influence and shape the decisions day after day, taken by management at all levels all through the organisation.

Here are three of Ric Willmot's Strategy Salvo's

1. Values should be seen not just heard
The General Manager of a multi-national company explained to me that he didn't approve of the vicious behaviour of one of his Sales Managers, infamous for offensively cudgelling sales representatives in open meetings. "But you do approve, David," I replied, " because your failure to do anything about it shows others that Peter's behaviour is the way to succeed here. Not only that, but you are developing mini Peters, and losing quality people who do not feel comfortable in this culture." Peter was terminated from the company within a month, but the clones took over a year to be converted or exited.

2. Values should be memorable
Values and vision must be concise enough to be used as daily templates for decision making and planning. All businesses make or lose money each day as the result of decisions made by employees. Lexus had a mission statement that was the equivalent of "Beat Benz." Komatsu, the heavy equipment manufacturer had one that basically said, "Eat Cat" referring to their rival Caterpillar. You want your employees to have it in their minds every day on the job, or else they won't be using them to guide decisions and take actions to support the business.

3. The Buck Stops at the Top
Salespeople, warehouse staff and customer service operators are held accountable for their sales, the speed and accuracy of deliveries, and their customer satisfaction. As we climb the hierarchical stairs, measures should become more difficult not easier. Business leaders must be made responsible for the company's future, quality and results. The helmsman may technically steer the ship, but the captain sets the destination. Navigators simply recommend the best course. The captain is responsible to the ships' owners and to those who sail in it.

If your SME has no strategy, how will you know where you are headed and what are the correct business decisions? If your SME doesn't break free from the negative behaviours that impact upon your business reputation, how might you expect to be treated seriously by the global audience you're trying to attract?

There are four basic patterns of thinking about your business:

1. What's going on? Get clarification and look objectively at the strategy you have operating currently.
2. Why is the business the way it is? The cause and effect analysis. Accumulate the knowledge you require to be even more successful than you currently are. Move beyond mere reaction to the environment, to make use of the environment.
3. Which course of action should you take? Allow for choice and give yourself options.
4. What lies ahead? What might be the future? Test arguments and philosophies, and search for positive instances as well as counter examples with critical thinking.

Recently, I watched a disturbing documentary about the famine in Africa. This program showed the Chiredzi District in Zimbabwe, where unfortunate people scrambled to the aid vehicles clamouring for much-needed food and drinking water. The current economic climate has caused many SME businesses to similarly scramble, grasping at and accepting business that is not the ideal type of work. Desperation has suppressed strategic discretion, and fear has overcome confidence to stay the course.

The successful organisations that have weathered the economic tsunami as it washed around the globe are the ones that diligently remained true to their strategic intent and implemented decisions that maintained the integrity of their previously determined plans.

It's always stressful with the rent due next week, but taking whatever business you can get, doesn't make an awful lot of sense if it is not your ideal type of work. We need to stop feeling sorry for ourselves and realise that the economy will improve, and we should be ahead of the curve to take advantage, else our competitors will.

However, many SMEs have never articulated who is their ideal client.
- do you know what is your ideal client-profile?
- what do those customers care about?
- what are their challenges?
- where are the opportunities for them?
- how could their business be improved by having you?

So, how do we intelligently grow our business? Start by cancelling the hunt. Yes, it's counterintuitive, with all the gurus waxing lyrical about 'hunters and farmers'. Hunting can be successful – there will always be white pointer sharks preying on seals, and the whale's greater threat is Japanese fishing boats, not an inability to win the battle against a giant squid. But these predators are successful only one out of twenty times. That's a hard day at the office.

Out-market your competition by focusing on what they are not. Your message to your ideal customer must be exciting. Provide real news to grab their attention and have a compelling call to action - a reason to respond. Right now, the marketplace is bored, frightened and confused. The marketplace is looking for their "Donald Trump" to shake up the establishment and bring about some change that is meaningful to them. Your organisation must project confidence, personality and even some attitude. Fervent, zealous people create compelling messages; what provides you with the most zeal

Focus on the outcomes you provide to your customers in terms of dramatic and valuable business results. What will your customers need to hear from you in order to buy? Take distinctive market positions by meeting unmet customer needs and afford them a better experience by buying from you. All of this does require courage and persistence. It requires the strength of will to rid yourself of the presumptions, assumptions, and industry rules. Instead of hunkering down in the trenches with your competitors, take the high ground and charge into the fray, awash with credibility and visibility for your value.

Maximise what you already do well, multiply the opportunities available and don't let the poor experiences of the recent past cause you to scramble for second-rate business. Those organisations that are well positioned will profit faster and better than those who are continuing to think in a reductionary manner.

It's easy to fall into the trap of thinking you need to be prettier if you want to be an actor. It turns out, though, that most important thespians aren't conventionally pretty (Marlon Brando, Clint Eastwood, Bette Davis, Geena Davis, Morgan Freeman). It's easy for an SME to believe that the best way to succeed is to be cheaper. However, just about every important brand (and every successful SME) didn't get that way by being the cheapest. Moreover, anyone who has been through business school has been reminded how important it is to be well-rounded. But, Nobel Prize winners, successful NGO founders and just about everyone you admire didn't get that way by being mediocre at many things.

We are not jellyfish floating on the waves, subject to tides and winds. SME enterprises have propulsive power if you choose to use it: resourcefulness, intellect and experience. You get a sense of the opportunity before us; for there is a rising tide of potential unless we wish to be a victim of the water.

Ric Willmot *is the author of 8 books and a global consultant. The owner of Executive Wisdom Consulting Group (http://executivewisdom.com), he is engaged by companies like Air Niugini, Motor Vehicle Insurance Limited, and CPA PNG to share his expertise and knowledge in improving organisational results. You may contact Ric at info@executivewisdom.com*

Leadership Training

Leadership Power
Mastering Leadership for a More Effective & Dynamic Organisation

All programs are designed, written and produced to your organisation's specific requirements.

What You Will Learn

This seminar course is designed for anyone who is currently in a leadership or managerial role and who would like to develop greater effectiveness in leading and motivating organisations and people. This program was developed in 2004 (under the title: *Awaken the Leadership Genius Within*) and has been tightly redefined and explicitly updated for 2018 and beyond. You will examines the multi-dimensional profile of modern leaders and develops critical behaviours associated with exemplary leaders.

Are your leadership skills useful in producing results for your organisation? Do you lead by example? Do you have effective leaders in your workplace? Master the different levels of management and leadership through developing your skills as a leader. This course will empower you to make the best decisions and achieve immeasurable results through effective leadership. You will discover how to create great teams to take your organisation to a higher level of efficiency and dynamism.

Every one of our training programs is uniquely designed and tailored to meet your specific circumstances and objectives.

Topic Menu includes but is not limited to:

- Why is leadership important?
- Getting to grips with leadership. What it really involves.
- How to develop the qualities, character traits and skills required to be an effective leader.
- Exploding the leadership myths.
- There is no *one* correct leadership style: Leadership styles and how to adapt as necessary.
- The different types of leadership required in any organisation and why different situations need unique guidance.
- Flexibility and adaptability — improved capability.
- Consequences of leadership: Are you prepared?
- Leadership in action and how to inspire the best from people.
- Understand how to energise and motivate others through your personal direction.
- The secrets to building high-performance teams and how to motivate them to achieve their best.
- Managing in times of change and stress. How to initiate change, navigate through the challenges and get lasting results.
- Managing relationships more effectively.
- Alignment and clarity.
- When things go wrong, here's what to do to get back on track fast and avoid losing the confidence of your team.
- The right way to use delegation both to improve results and be a more effective leader.

How You Will Stand to Benefit as an Organisation

For any great organisation, the people are its most valuable asset. Your people are employed to achieve your business goals. *The Executive Wisdom Leadership Power* training is an essential enabler for bringing out the best in your team. Business benefits as reported by previous course attendees include:

- Greatly enhanced business performance and results as the result of improved leadership in your organisation.
- Your staff will not only perform better but will be more satisfied due to more transparent, apparent, and explicit leadership and direction.
- A more flexible and adaptable organisation, able to deal with change more effectively.
- Your managers will be better equipped to deal with challenges and experience less stress.
- An enhanced business reputation as your company and people stand out for exercising greater leadership.

Who Benefits from this Course?

This course is specifically designed to take managers at any stage of their career to a new and higher level of leadership skill and power. We've had hundreds of people of varying skill levels from new managers to CEOs from many different industry verticals attend the course. Both the individuals and the companies sending them on the course experience the benefits of the training. This course is recommended for:

- New Managers
- Experienced Managers taking on new responsibilities
- Senior Staff and Role Models
- Project Team Leaders
- Executive Management
- Senior Managers & Department Heads
- C-suite executives

We customise- the course to every level and audience depending on your requirements.

How is this Course Delivered?

After an initial consultation with your organisation, we will assess the skill level of the group and the desired business results you need. We then customise the training. You will save your organisation's time, resources and money by us coming to you and delivering the training at your premises or a location determined to be ideal for your needs and desired outcomes. The Leadership Power training course, based on your requirements, ranges from two to four days.

How many Delegates can Attend?

Typically, we suggest a maximum of 24 people from your organisation attend the training at any one time. This limit is suggested because of the *hands on* nature of the training and the individual feedback given to each person attending the training. Larger groups can be accommodated, however, and we can structure the training to best meet your requirements.

Leadership Training

Transformational Leadership
How Leaders Can Effect Successful Change in Companies, Organisations, and Teams

All programs are designed, written and produced to your organisation's specific requirements.

What You Will Learn

This course deepens your understanding of how leaders produce change in organisations. Specifically, how leaders establish a compelling direction, align people and groups, and inspire and motivate them to achieve common goals. The course begins by examining certain myths about leadership, including the notion that leaders are born, not made. You will evaluate different conceptions of leadership, as well as various theoretical models. You will discover that all successful leaders do *not* have a common set of personality traits. The course embraces the notion that certain leaders are suited for particular situations and that leaders at times must adapt their style to fit the needs of specific circumstances.

We examine why individuals and organisations resist change, looking specifically at how people often respond rigidly to situations perceived as threatening to them. The course examines the critical steps in a successful transformation process. Leaders must articulate a compelling vision that includes ambitious stretch goals. However, achieving small wins proves crucial in moving an organisation along the path toward those goals. Ultimately, leaders must ensure that changes "stick" in a team and special techniques can be used to help institutionalise change. To build organisations that endure, leaders must foster an environment of continuous improvement and innovation. Leaders have to develop and guide learning processes, and they have to foster environments that are conducive to creativity and innovation.

Every one of our training programs is uniquely designed and tailored to meet your specific circumstances and objectives.

Topic Menu includes but is not limited to:

- The challenge of transformational leadership.
- Portrait of a Transformation.
- Do great leaders share the same traits?
- How much does context matter?
- Charismatic and Transformational Leadership.
- Resistance and reactions to change.
- Phases of Transformation.
- Making change stick.
- Extrinsic Motivation and Reward.
- Beyond money—Intrinsic Motivation.
- Power —Understanding it, getting it, and keeping it.
- Key Levers of Power.
- Influence—Tools of Persuasion.
- Avoiding the zero sum game.
- Building and leading teams.
- Guiding teams as they evolve.
- Observation and Organisational Learning.
- Stimulating creativity.
- Leading Innovation.
- Developing Leaders.

How You Will Stand to Benefit as an Organisation

To produce lasting change, transformational leaders must become adept at motivating, persuading, and influencing others. At times, leaders must accumulate and exercise power in organisations to get things done. Business benefits as reported by previous course attendees include:

- Learning the subtle approaches of influence and persuasion.
- How to negotiate in a complex organisation and with multiple stakeholders to achieve the corporate objectives.
- Understanding the dynamics of team composition, guiding groups during critical stages of their development, and facilitating decision-making processes.
- How to achieve corporate goals through teams of people while avoiding GroupThink, and being aware of the possibility that a group can fracture into opposing camps at times.
- How effective leaders develop the people who work for them, and they cultivate their successors.

Who Benefits from this Course?

This course is specifically designed to take leaders and managers to a new and higher level of change and transformational leadership skill and power. We've had hundreds of people of varying skill levels from new managers to CEOs from many different industry verticals attend the course. Both the individuals and the companies sending them on the course experience the benefits of the training. This course is recommended for:

- New Managers
- Experienced Managers taking on new responsibilities
- HR personnel
- Senior Staff and Role Models
- Team Leaders & Supervisors
- Middle Management
- Executive Management
- Senior Managers & Department Heads
- C-suite executives
- Board members
- Business owners

We customise- the course to every level and audience depending on your requirements.

How is this Course Delivered?

After an initial consultation with your organisation, we will assess the skill level of the group and the desired business results you need. We then customise the training. You will save your organisation's time, resources and money by us coming to you and delivering the training at your premises or a location determined to be ideal for your needs and desired outcomes. The Transformational Leadership training course, based on your requirements, ranges from two to five days.

How many Delegates can Attend?

Typically, we suggest a maximum of 24 people from your organisation attend the training at any one time. This limit is suggested because of the *hands on* nature of the training and the individual feedback given to each person attending the training. Larger groups can be accommodated, however, and we can structure the training to best meet your requirements.

Strategic Management Training

Strategic Thinking Skills

Unravelling chaos and harnessing the power of your organisation to improve results

All programs are designed, written and produced to your organisation's specific requirements.

What You Will Learn

Strategy is not a ready-made plan we can pull from a shelf, nor is it a tool we can take from a toolbox. This course deepens your understanding of how to overcome both internal and external obstacles that block the way to achieving our goals. The framework for strategic thinking is a series of powerful analytical tools that enable us to make sense of a complex world and can transform the way we think, behave, and interact with others. You will examine how strategic dynamism suffuses and revolutionises your thinking in other realms of endeavour and is an indispensable tool in the worlds of the military, business, politics, sports, and even entertainment.

Regardless of the area of endeavour, the key to any successful strategy is an overall sense of mission. You learn the fundamental competitive choices that are available, their advantages and disadvantages, and how to position your organisation for the most successful strategic outcomes. You also learn the sources of competitive advantage and the superb technique: blue ocean strategy. We analyse the incredible utility of the intelligence cycle and scenario planning as engines of predictive capability, predictive of both the specific likely actions of competitors and the likely course of macro-factors that can affect our plans.

Key to the success or failure of much strategic action, is the mindset of the strategist. You will investigate cognitive psychology, strategic intuition, game theory, systemic problems, and perspectives on "luck" demonstrate that our own self-perception and the perception of the world around us can have a tremendous impact on the effectiveness of our strategy.

Every one of our training programs is uniquely designed and tailored to meet your specific circumstances and objectives.

Topic Menu includes but is not limited to:

- The Dawn of Strategic Thinking.
- Modern Principles of Strategic Conflict.
- Grand Strategists and Strategic Intent.
- The Core of Strategic Planning.
- Fundamental Choices: Which Strategy?
- Competitive Advantage: Blue Ocean.
- SWOT.
- Avoid the Pathologies of Execution.
- Perils and power of Strategic Deception.
- Move & Countermove: Game Theory.
- The Evolution of Cooperation.
- When Strategy Breaks Down.
- Leveraging Cognitive Psychology.
- Strategic Intuition and Creative Insight.
- Systematic Problems to Systematic Solutions.
- Seize the future with Scenario Analysis.
- The correlation of forces, luck, and culture.
- Strategic Thinking as a way of life.

How You Will Stand to Benefit as an Organisation

You will comprehend how to utilise the tools of analysis and tactics to take decisive and prudent action that affords the best possible opportunity of achieving your objectives. Business benefits as reported by previous course attendees include:

- Learning the process of mission, objective, situation analysis, strategy formulation, strategy implementation, and control.
- How to constantly evaluate the external and internal environments and modify your strategy according to arising needs.
- Understanding the principles of strategic thinking and the potential rewards awaiting those who cultivate strategic thinking skills as a way of life.
- How to achieve corporate goals through understanding not to fear the future but harness its potential for the organisation's benefit.
- How to see patterns and routines, to identify categories, and to sense the broader macro-shifts in a particular correlation of forces that affect your organisation in unique ways.
- By adopting various combinations of techniques and tools of analysis, this course on strategic thinking provides clarity and efficacy of action in a forever changing and chaotic world.

Who Benefits from this Course?

This course is specifically designed to take leaders and accomplished managers and improve their strategic thinking and strategy planning. People of varying skill levels up to and including CEOs and board members from many different industry verticals attend the course. Both the individuals and the companies sending them on the course experience the benefits of the training. This course is recommended for:

- Experienced Managers taking on new responsibilities
- Senior Staff and Role Models
- Team Leaders & Supervisors
- Senior Management
- Executive Management
- Department Heads
- C-suite executives
- Board members
- Business owners

We customise- the course to every level and audience depending on your requirements.

How is this Course Delivered?

After an initial consultation with your organisation, we will assess the objectives, goals, and the desired business results you need. We then customise the training. You will save your organisation's time, resources and money by us coming to you and delivering the training at your premises or a location determined to be ideal for your needs and desired outcomes. The Strategic Thinking Skills training course, based on your requirements, ranges from two to three days.

How many Delegates can Attend?

Typically, we suggest a maximum of 24 people from your organisation attend the training at any one time. This limit is suggested because of the *hands on* nature of the training and the individual feedback given to each person attending the training. Larger groups can be accommodated, however, and we can structure the training to best meet your requirements.

Strategic Management Training

Strategy Unwrapped
Strategic Thinking, Planning, & Implementation in a Volatile Market

All programs are designed, written and produced to your organisation's specific requirements.

What You Will Learn

Strategic success is the holy grail of owner-principals, CEOs, partners, and senior executives. However, the challenges of an ever-increasing competitiveness mean that the shrug-and-smile approach to delivering on business objectives has all but vanished. Today's business leaders have to account for: global and local competition, organisational resilience, staffing shortages, increased risk and uncertainty, accelerating social, economic and technological change.

Despite strategy being the most potent ingredient for superior performance, very few organisations manage the strategic process well. They have to deal with an uncertain world where the only certainty in a plan is that events will never follow the plan. In this highly interactive program, you will improve your understanding on which dimensions of business link strategy to activities. To not only survive but thrive in an uncertain world requires creating and setting a plan that people can use because action is the only precursor to success.

If you want to learn real-world strategy, not just textbook theory; understand what really happens in the boardroom, in the executive suite and on the front line where the workers have to make it happen; and learn what you need to know to become a supercharged strategy specialist, then you have to request this program be conducted in your organisation by the advisor, coach, and mentor of many senior executives in Fortune 1000 companies around the world.

Every one of our training programs is uniquely designed and tailored to meet your specific circumstances and objectives.

Topic Menu includes but is not limited to:

- Which business strategy?
- Your competitive advantage.
- Modern principles of strategic conflict.
- Avoid the pathologies of execution.
- Move and countermove — Game Theory.
- Overcoming the failure of existing strategy.
- Strength of leadership when strategy breaks down.
- Perils and power of strategic deception.
- Why strategy is not a template.
- Pre-empting problems and what to do about them.
- Behavioural economics and its impact on strategic thinking.
- Why our brains are designed to succeed, and why our brains are programmed to make us fail.
- Strategic intuition and creative insight.
- Seize the future with scenario analysis.
- Groupthink — Thinking or conforming?
- The wisdom of crowds.

How You Will Stand to Benefit as an Organisation

You will comprehend how to create a strategy that can be implemented, and learn to articulate your strategy to be understood and appreciated. Benefits as reported by previous course attendees include:

- Learning how to establish organisational objectives to enhance growth and implement the strategy to achieve buy-in from major stakeholders.
- How to constantly evaluate the external and internal environments and modify your strategy according to arising needs.
- Understanding how to develop the necessary actions, teams, processes, and evaluation tools needed to manage strategy and the change that happens as a result.
- How to integrate and link various components of management to make informed decisions.
- You will be exposed to the leading concept of behavioural economics and its impact on strategic thinking.
- You will recognise the psychological factors of your environment and how it affects group dynamics.

Who Benefits from this Course?

This course is specifically designed to take leaders and accomplished managers and improve their strategic thinking and strategy planning. People of varying skill levels up to and including CEOs and board members from many different industry verticals attend the course. Both the individuals and the companies sending them on the course experience the benefits of the training. This course is recommended for:

- Experienced Managers taking on new responsibilities
- Senior Staff and Role Models
- Team Leaders & Supervisors
- Senior Management
- Executive Management
- Department Heads
- C-suite executives
- Board members
- Business owners

We customise- the course to every level and audience depending on your requirements.

How is this Course Delivered?

After an initial consultation with your organisation, we will assess the objectives, goals, and the desired business results you need. We then customise the training. You will save your organisation's time, resources and money by us coming to you and delivering the training at your premises or a location determined to be ideal for your needs and desired outcomes. The Strategy Unwrapped training course, based on your requirements, ranges from two to three days.

How many Delegates can Attend?

Typically, we suggest a maximum of 40 people from your organisation attend the training at any one time. This limit is suggested because of the *hands on* nature of the training and the individual feedback given to each person attending the training. Larger groups can be accommodated, however, and we can structure the training to best meet your requirements.

Management Training

Art of Conflict Management
How to Effect Successful Resolutions in Companies, Organisations, and Teams

All programs are designed, written and produced to your organisation's specific requirements.

What You Will Learn

Conflict occurs in all human relationships. Mishandled, it harms individuals, interpersonal relationships, organisations, communities, and nations. Handled well, it helps identify and solve problems and build stronger, deeper relationships. Throughout human history, cultures, governments, tribes, and organisations have developed mores and rules for handling conflict with the intention of limiting the harm conflict can do and securing the benefits of stable and productive relationships.

In this course you will make a concerted effort to understand conflict better and develop helpful ways to manage it. You will study different conflict styles, some much more effective than others, and describe specific ways to manage conflict and negotiate agreements more successfully—with less damage and more gain. You will look at the pivotal role of managers in dealing with conflict in the workplace and devote time to understanding how and where to get and give help in managing conflicts.

Throughout the learning of this course, you will understand that conflict in organisations is normal and inescapable. Knowing that, conflict is an opportunity to understand opposing preferences and values. It's energy that can either help or damage your organisation and your people. Unfortunately, if dysfunctional strategies are utilised, some damage is irreversible. For these reasons, The Art of Conflict Management training course is a program that any and all organisations should embrace for all staff.

"In itself, conflict is not a problem ... it's how we handle it that makes the difference."

Every one of our training programs is uniquely designed and tailored to meet your specific circumstances and objectives.

Topic Menu includes but is not limited to:

- Why Conflict Management Matters.
- The Adversary System.
- Perception, Perspective, & Punctuation.
- Managing Multiple and Conflicting Emotions.
- Multiple, Complex, and Changing Goals.
- Power—How Much We Need and How to Use It.
- Conflict Styles.
- Dysfunctional Conflict Strategies.
- Principled Negotiation.
- Preparing and Arranging to Negotiate.
- Negotiating Conflict Resolutions.
- How Management Theories Affect Conflict.
- The Manager's Role in Dealing with Conflict.
- Helping Others Manage Conflict.
- Moral and Cultural Conflicts.
- Managing Conflict's Aftermath.
- Conflict Management—A Success in Progress.

How You Will Stand to Benefit as an Organisation

The primary aim of this course is to offer new insights into the nature of conflict and the challenges and opportunities conflicts present. Business benefits as reported by previous course attendees include:

- Learning to understand the nature of conflict, including the roles of perspective, emotions, goals, and power.
- How to gain an appreciation of the serious efforts to find more effective ways to manage conflict.
- Understanding that conflict is normal and indicates an organisation is growing and developing.
- Learning how conflict deepens and improves relationships when it is handled appropriately.
- How the perception of conflict is a major reason for the trouble of conflict in organisations.

Who Benefits from this Course?

This course is for anyone in organisational life who wishes to improve their strategies and techniques in conflict management. We've had hundreds of people of varying skill levels from new managers to CEOs from many different industry verticals attend the course. Both the individuals and the companies sending them on the course experience the benefits of the training. This course is recommended for:

- New Managers
- Experienced Managers taking on new responsibilities
- HR personnel
- Senior Staff and Role Models
- Team Leaders & Supervisors
- Middle Management
- Executive Management
- Senior Managers & Department Heads
- C-suite executives
- Board members
- Business owners

We customise- the course to every level and audience depending on your requirements.

How is this Course Delivered?

We fine-tune and customise this program for your organisation's training needs. You will save your organisation's time, resources and money by us coming to you and delivering the training at your premises or a location determined to be ideal for your needs and desired outcomes. The Art of Conflict Management training course, is usually two days in length.

How many Delegates can Attend?

Typically, we suggest a maximum of 40 people from your organisation attend the training at any one time. This is a highly engaging and interactive training program. Larger groups can be accommodated, however, and we can structure the training to best meet your requirements.

Working with Ric has been a great experience as he is a passionate mentor and trainer. With so much positive feedback from his training programs, I know that Ric is not only knowledgeable, creative, and professional but he consistently delivers new ideas and development in his courses. His training is filled with relevant subjects, well-planned delivery, and packed with fun and motivating elements for all levels of management professional. As our trainer, Ric has always been very supportive of our marketing activities with ideas and tools in delivering better solutions to our clients. Working together these few years has also given us the opportunities to practise Ric's business acumen and tools internally within our organisation. His business insights and professionalism prove valuable to everyone that has been attending his training and many others to come. A great person, trainer, coach, and mentor ... and a friend: Ric Willmot!

— **Hani Sidek, Director of Insumo Limited, UK | Malaysia**

Leadership & Management Training

Leading Organisational Change & Transformation

How to Transform Your Organisation to Survive and Prosper in an Age of Disruption

All programs are designed, written and produced to your organisation's specific requirements.

What You Will Learn

Executive Wisdom are specialists in change management consulting and training. So much so that Ric Willmot has been engaged more than 70 times in the last 10 years to deliver Change & Transformation programs in Australia, Brunei, Fiji, Hong Kong, Indonesia, Malaysia, New Zealand, Papua New Guinea, Philippines, Singapore, South Africa, South Korea, Thailand, United Arab Emirates, and United States. This comprehensive course forces you to consider what constitutes change within the context of the current economic and social environment of your organisation. It covers how individuals are likely to react to change, based on their role, experience, personal demographics (including personality and cultural differences) – and crucially, the part of the manager in developing a management plan and communication strategy that most ably facilitates the smooth running of change in your organisation.

We will address a broad spectrum of transformational leadership, continuous improvement, and change management techniques and strategies. This unique course is designed with critical information on how to use transformation and change management in your organisation. You will develop a deep understanding of the methodologies that produce positive results, and learn how to execute them in the business world to achieve better and longer-lasting outcomes. By understanding and engaging the concepts and tactics taught, organisations will stop making costly mistakes, and improve performance.

Topic Menu includes but is not limited to:

- Why is Change Management important?
- Assessing the necessity for change.
- Why Executive Sponsorship is a Critical Success Factor.
- Checklist for Resistance to Change.
- The Psychological Environment.
- Overcoming the popular mistakes and causes of failure.
- Tools, diagnostics and instruments for creating successful, long-lived change.
- Five behavioural factors to successful influence and manage stakeholders.
- Understanding the Change Models — which will work best for you?
- Force Field Analysis Extended—working with your employee-groups.
- Life Cycle Questionnaire — an indicator of organisational effectiveness.
- Next-Level Change & Transformational Leadership.
- Improving Your Success in Change by Eliminating Execution Failures.
- Communicating the Change Vision.
- Anchoring new approaches in culture.
- Evaluating your progress to minimise collateral damage and remain focused on the objective.
- Reinforcing change in support of operational success.

How You Will Stand to Benefit as an Organisation

The primary aim of this course is to guide managers and leaders to implement organisational change and lead transformation. Business benefits as reported by previous course attendees include:

- Achieving the ability to implement the skills and behaviours of any role in change management.
- Accelerating the implementation of transformation and change to support the application of business improvement.
- Learning effective communication styles to deal with interpersonal conflicts that automatically arise during periods of transition and growth.
- Recognising the opportunities presented by change and learning how to take advantage of them.
- Benchmarking change management strategies and performance with leading institutions.

Who Benefits from this Course?

This course is for anyone in organisational life who wishes to improve their strategies and techniques in change management and transformational leadership. We've had hundreds of people of varying skill levels from new managers to CEOs from many different industry verticals attend the course. Both the individuals and the companies sending them on the course experience the benefits of the training. This course is recommended for:

- New Managers
- Experienced Managers taking on new responsibilities
- HR personnel
- Senior Staff and Role Models
- Team Leaders & Supervisors
- Middle Management
- Executive Management
- Senior Managers & Department Heads
- C-suite executives
- Board members
- Business owners

We customise- the course to every level and audience depending on your requirements.

How is this Course Delivered?

We fine-tune and customise this program for your organisation's training needs. You will save your organisation's time, resources and money by us coming to you and delivering the training at your premises or a location determined to be ideal for your needs and desired outcomes. The Leading Organisational Change & Transformation training course, based on your requirements, ranges from two to four days.

How many Delegates can Attend?

Typically, we suggest a maximum of 30 people from your organisation attend the training at any one time. This is a highly engaging and interactive training program. Larger groups can be accommodated, however, and we can structure the training to best meet your requirements.

Ric Willmot's seminar exceeded my expectations! We learned the principles of how to apply management skills to our business and make an immediate impact. This was a very insightful experience with intensive workshop instruction and practice with high quality and comprehensive support materials. I enthusiastically recommend such training to others who wish to raise the bar on business management skills.
— **Yuwak Tau, Executive Director of CPA PNG**

Leadership & Management Training

Critical Decision Making
How to Effect Better, Successful Decisions in Companies, Organisations, and Teams

All programs are designed, written and produced to your organisation's specific requirements.

What You Will Learn

Why did that leader make such a horrible decision? We have all asked that question when we have observed a poor decision, whether it be in politics, business, athletics, or the non-profit sector. Too often, observers attribute such flawed choices to incompetence, inexperience, a lack of intelligence, or bad intentions. In most cases, though, the wrong decisions do not arise because of these factors.

In this course, we examine why leaders and organisations make poor choices, digging deep into cognitive psychology, group dynamics, and theories of organisational culture and systems to help us understand why well-intentioned, capable people blunder. Moreover, we examine the techniques and behaviours that leaders can employ to improve decision making in their organisation. We focus on how leaders can design decision-making processes that marshal the collective intellect in their organisations, bringing together the diverse expertise, perspectives, and talents to determine the best course of action.

The course uses case studies to examine decision making at three levels: individual, group, and organisational. We examine how individuals make choices. We show that most individuals do not examine every possible alternative or collect enough information and data when making choices. Instead, most of us draw on our experience, apply rules of thumb, and use other heuristics when making decisions. As it turns out, most individuals are susceptible to what psychologists call cognitive biases—decision traps that cause us to make certain systematic mistakes when making choices.

Every one of our training programs is uniquely designed and tailored to meet your specific circumstances and objectives.

Topic Menu includes but is not limited to:

- Making High-Stakes Decisions.
- Cognitive Biases.
- Avoiding Decision-Making Traps.
- Framing—Risk or Opportunity?
- Intuition—Recognising Patterns.
- Reasoning by Analogy.
- Making Sense of Ambiguous Situations.
- The Wisdom of Crowds?
- Groupthink—Thinking or Conforming?
- Deciding How to Decide.
- Stimulating Conflict and Debate.
- Keeping Conflict Constructive.
- Creativity and Brainstorming.
- The Curious Inability to Decide.
- Achieving Closure through Small Wins.
- Normal Accident Theory.
- Normalising Deviance.
- Three Lenses.
- Practical Drift.
- Ambiguous Threats and the Recovery Window.
- Connecting the Dots.
- Seeking Out Problems.
- Asking the Right Questions.

How You Will Stand to Benefit as an Organisation

The primary aim of this course is to guide managers and leaders to make better, more successful organisational decisions. Business benefits as reported by previous course attendees include:

- Learning that intuition represents a powerful pattern-recognition capability that individuals have, drawing from their wealth of experience. However, intuition can lead us astray, and this course explains how and why that can happen, particularly when we reason by analogy.
- We examine how teams make decisions, recognising that most of us do not make all our choices on our own. Instead, we often work in groups to make complex choices.
- We discuss the problems that typically arise, such as groupthink—that is, the tendency for groups to experience powerful pressures for conformity, which suppress dissenting views and lead to clouded judgments.
- We also examine why teams often find themselves riddled with indecision. Most importantly, we examine how groups can stimulate constructive conflict, as well as achieve consensus and timely closure so that they can overcome these problems and make better decisions.
- Leaders must behave differently to improve decision making in their organisations. Specifically, leaders have to dispel the notion that they must have all the answers to tough problems. Instead, they must view their responsibility as designing the decision-making processes that help the organisation make better choices. Leaders have to create productive dialogues in their organisations, and to do so, they have to understand the pitfalls that are described in this course, as well as the techniques that can be used to enhance decision-making effectiveness.

Who Benefits from this Course?

This course is for anyone in organisational life who wishes to improve their strategies and techniques in decision making. We've had hundreds of people of varying skill levels from new managers to CEOs from many different industry verticals attend the course. Both the individuals and the companies sending them on the course experience the benefits of the training. This course is recommended for:

- New Managers
- Experienced Managers taking on new responsibilities
- HR personnel
- Senior Staff and Role Models
- Team Leaders & Supervisors
- Middle Management
- Executive Management
- Senior Managers & Department Heads
- C-suite executives
- Board members
- Business owners

We customise- the course to every level and audience depending on your requirements.

How is this Course Delivered?

We fine-tune and customise this program for your organisation's training needs. You will save your organisation's time, resources and money by us coming to you and delivering the training at your premises or a location determined to be ideal for your needs and desired outcomes. The Critical Decision Making training course, based on your requirements, ranges from two to three days.

How many Delegates can Attend?

Typically, we suggest a maximum of 30 people from your organisation attend the training at any one time. This is a highly engaging and interactive training program. Larger groups can be accommodated, however, and we can structure the training to best meet your requirements.

Leadership & Management Training

4-Day Program: Senior Management Transformation

Managing Organisational Change, Business Transformation, Stakeholder Engagement, and Communications

All programs are designed, written and produced to your organisation's specific requirements.

What You Will Learn

Senior executives often know that business transformation and organisational change is imperative but are unable to determine precisely what has to change or how to make it happen. Added to this, many do not understand how to implement a successful organisational change strategy and communicate it effectively to their stakeholders.

The problem is most companies are unable to define a clear strategy and vision for transformation and change. Moreover, they are hindered by an inadequate stakeholder engagement plan and ineffective communication strategy. Without the best strategies to handle this, organisations may face poor transformation process and miscommunication among stakeholders and employees, thus hindering successful business transformation, improvement and growth.

This course helps set you in the right direction for a transformational initiative and thereby inspire effective action. This program will redefine how you think about change management in your organisation and spur you to embark on your change management journey. This comprehensive 4-day program, designed for CEO and senior management executives, will show you how to execute successful business transformation, organisational change, and effectively engage your stakeholders with persuasive communication techniques. You will learn the different models of change management and tools that you can apply to lead changes more efficiently.

You examine people's attitudes and assumptions towards change and build an effective stakeholder engagement and communications plan to create and sustain a positive momentum for change while forming a broad network of support. You will discover the critical steps you should adopt when undertaking strategic change management and establish an action plan that will help you commit people to action. Through actual case studies and group discussions, you will understand why up to 70% of change initiatives fail, the critical success drivers that underpin a successful change, and how you can embark on an effective change journey today.

Every one of our training programs is uniquely designed and tailored to meet your specific circumstances and objectives.

Topic Menu includes but is not limited to:

- Why is transformation so important? What's the ROI?
- HR implementing the latest fad does not guarantee improved organisational performance.
- What's your objective? How will your organisation benefit? Will this be the most efficacious process to achieve your desired results?
- Assessing the necessity for change and transformation.
- Forced change by: competitors, consumers, government, economic climate, technology, etc.
- Escaping the doldrums.
- Deliberate change to raise the bar.
- A focus on the future: Clarifying future direction and organisational strategy.
- How to optimise enterprise resources, minimise fragmentation and resource dilution.
- Create an environment for successful change initiatives.
- Identify barriers and solutions to eliminate or minimise the negatives of change initiatives.
- Transformation is an organic process, not a single event.
- Problem solving or innovation creation?
- Why Executive Sponsorship is a Critical Success Factor.
- Who are the key people within your organisation you must get on board?
- Resistor, neutral, supporter — what they do and how you should respond.
- Developing an exemplar culture.
- Assessing the psychological environment for change & transformation.
- Checklist for Resistance to Change.
- Strategies to overcome the reasons for people resisting change.
- Overcoming the popular mistakes and causes of failure.
- Differentiating between myth and reality.
- The antibiotic is fine, it's the diagnosis that was wrong.
- Five behavioural factors to influence and manage stakeholders.
- The psychology of powerful performance in people.
- Understanding the Change Models.
- Just because one model worked for them doesn't mean it will work for you.
- You have to know your objective before you can choose your change model.
- Force Field Analysis Extended — Working with your employees to make them more effective.
- The Life Cycle Questionnaire — An indicator of organisational effectiveness.
- Improving your success by eliminating execution failures.
- Minimise the negative impact of blocked communication channels and information distortion.
- Organisational and stakeholder empowerment.
- Build an organisation that creates value for its stakeholders – investors, customers, suppliers and employees.
- Utilise the inter-related roles of board directors, executive management, and HR department.
- Anchoring new approaches in culture.
- The new way has to be programmed as the default position.

How You Will Stand to Benefit as an Organisation

By the end of this program, participants will be able to:
- Accelerate the implementation of transformation and change to support the application of business improvement.
- Learn effective communication styles to deal with interpersonal conflicts that inevitably arise during periods of transition and growth.
- Recognise the opportunities presented by change and learn how to take advantage of them.
- Build understanding, trust, and co-operation between internal and external stakeholders.
- Build a learning organisation that is agile and adapts to rapid change.

Who Benefits from this Course?

This course is for anyone in organisational life who wishes to improve their strategies and techniques in decision making. We've had hundreds of people of varying skill levels from new managers to CEOs from many different industry verticals attend the course. Both the individuals and the companies sending them on the course experience the benefits of the training. This course is recommended for:

- Project Managers
- Continuous Improvement Managers
- HR and Operational Excellence staff
- QA & BPR
- Team Leaders & Supervisors
- Change Team Leaders
- Business Transformation
- Executive Management
- Senior Managers & Department Heads
- C-suite executives
- Board members
- Business owners

We customise- the course to every level and audience depending on your requirements.

How is this Course Delivered?

We customise this program for your organisation's training needs. You will save your organisation's time, resources and money by us coming to you and delivering the training at your premises or a location determined to be ideal for your needs and desired outcomes. The Senior Management Transformation training course is best delivered as a 4-Day Executive Training course. Based on your requirements, the program ranges from three to five days.

How many Delegates can Attend?

Typically, we suggest a maximum of 24 people from your organisation attend the training at any one time. This is a highly engaging and interactive training program. Larger groups can be accommodated, however, and we can structure the training to best meet your requirements.

" The one blog that I ensure I read every day is Ric Wilmot's blog. Ric provides helpful hints, tips and support to business owners, managers and employees.

He has fantastic insights into how to extract the best from employees across every role in any sector. A true "must read" blog.

Michael Cosgrove - *River City Consulting*

Make customers come to you!

By Ric Willmot, Consultant and mentor, Executive Wisdom

Television, fiction books and experiences teach me more about business than do business books, primarily because most business books are lousy and shoddy, ranging from abstract vagaries to the subjective recollections of gurus stating "This is how I did it, you only need to emulate me".

I'm a TV addict who cannot get enough of documentaries on NatGeo, the History Channel and the Discovery Channel. A program that grabbed my attention was Walking with Dinosaurs. But what confused and created scepticism for me was when the legendary pre-historic T-Rex, faced several times in a hunt and intentionally left alone a cluster of herbivores for the reason that they were firmly planted in a defensive circle. Hold on! This is supposed to be the most ferocious carnivore in the history of alfresco dining! The narrator, anticipating my incredulousness, stated "less than 10% of predator attacks are successful today."

Recruitment professionals, in light of the low success rates of even the most lethal predator, and the analogous low success rates of sales approaches, should stop cold calls on unsuspecting prospects. My experience shows that the cold call fails 90% of the time.

Quit bitching

I hear this every day – prospects won't return your calls, they cancel meetings on the day, their secretary screens your mail and their company has a PSA with another organisation. There's no money and the tenant is wrong. Who cares?! We need to stop feeling sorry for ourselves and realise that cold calling is a low return sales technique.

Cancel the hunt

Yes, it is counter-intuitive, with all the gurus waxing lyrical about 'hunters and farmers'. Hunting can be successful – there will always be white pointers preying on seals. But these animals hunt intuitively for prey that is incapable of technological improvement. Okapi don't keep lions at bay by using voice mail, and evolution takes a tad longer than Facebook, Twitter or LinkedIn. No recruitment firm can build a growing organisation with hunting as the predominant sales technique, no matter how adept the owner, manager or BDM may be.

The modern business world has evolved biologically in favour of defense, not offence.

Effect on business growth?

Build a brand that compels buyers to come to you. Nobody walks into McDonald's to browse through the menu. Branding is the means to persuading buyers to seek you out and ask how you might be able to assist them. All that is left for you is to not inadvertently insult the buyer's dress sense and a deal is done.

I am regularly asked by both large recruitment firms and solo practitioners 'how can we differentiate ourselves from our competitors?' It is a legitimate issue.

Irresistible value proposition

- Ask your clients, past and present, what results you have delivered. For example, did you increase productivity by securing the best talent, reduce attrition through improved communications, or career development, or lower hiring costs through improved induction procedures?
- Decide what you are most passionate about. Compelling messages are created by fervent, zealous people.
- Create a brand around client outcomes about which you are passionate.
- Make use of the brand in every communication. Have it in your marketing collateral, on your website, in your email signature. Write about it, speak about it. This creates a whirlpool marketing effect, drawing buyers into your business centre.
- Encourage word of mouth. Don't just let this happen – make it happen!
- Become extremely user-friendly. Eliminate distractions, impediments, policies and procedures that annoy and confuse your clients and prospects.

Willmot's marketing whirlpool

You can embed in your brand equity through frequency, recency and front of mind. By regularly engaging in a whirlpool of activity you create gravity drawing business in to you rather than going out to seek the prospects and enquiries. Maintaining ongoing communications and information flow is very important. Public seminars, speaking opportunities, position papers, radio and press interviews and alliances establish credibility and visibility and place you as the 'go to' person in recruitment.

I'm convinced that the future for SMEs (it's already been proved for larger firms) is in convincing clients to come to them and that is successfully achieved through assertive branding. The predatory approach will work even less in the future because:

- Larger firms have more marketing resources and finance
- Telephone, hard-copy and electronic approaches are becoming tough to penetrate, and
- Despite technology, hunting is growing more expensive and SMEs have limited resources – especially time.

All predators ultimately yield to more effective and efficient predators, more evolved descendants or environmental change. I will surrender to the couple of exceptions, crocodiles and sharks, if you will surrender to the other 99% I am right about. The sabre-tooth tiger lost his reign and his existence.

Start improving your brand power and your ability to draw buyers to you today. However, be aware that any petition to 'hunt buyers' is followed effort, even shadowed to the minimal gain of successful hunting. That's why I watch television, much to the pundit's chagrin. I don't want to be hunting the herd. I want the herd to stop by my place.

Ric Willmot assists clients to increase performance and profit by making distinctive, lasting and substantial improvements to their organisations. He partners with his clients to tackle their most difficult issues and serious challenges. Ric's clients include PricewaterhouseCoopers, CPA Australia, Australian Legal Practice Management Association, Grant Thornton, and over 100 other leading organisations. Over 2000 people have joined his Private Mentoring and Coaching Program. He's been the CEO of three successful companies, one of which was a Brisbane-based HR and recruitment firm. Ric has now built a seven figure global consulting practice based in Brisbane.

Management Training

Business Negotiations Skills
The Art & Science of Negotiating the Best Deal

All programs are designed, written and produced to your organisation's specific requirements.

What You Will Learn

Few professional skills are as important as negotiation, and fewer still are as seemingly challenging. Most of us feel uneasy about negotiating, yet we know it is crucial. We negotiate whenever we buy a car, work out the terms of a new job, or resolve a complex business conflict. However, that is just the tip of the iceberg. Through this training course you'll acquire the ability to go far beyond merely doing well in one-time, arms-length transactions. The training program will challenge you to aspire to a greater vision of what you can achieve with excellent negotiating skills. In fact, having the ability to negotiate well can help you create more justice and prosperity for yourself and others. It can also help you become a better work colleague, manager, leader, and person.

In this course, you will see that negotiation is definitely a skill that can be learned. We explore a host of principles, skills, techniques, tools, and ideas that can dramatically improve your ability to negotiate. We investigate ways to cope with the many emotional aspects of negotiation that often seem so daunting. Moreover, far from fostering a selfish, short-sighted, and calculating approach, you will develop your ability to negotiate with integrity in principled, trustworthy ways.

You will explore a variety of advanced topics, including the emotions and psychological challenges of negotiations, cross-cultural negotiations, and negotiations with highly influential counterparts. You will learn ways to save and improve troubled agreements and explore a host of powerful and principled persuasion techniques.

Every one of our training programs is uniquely designed and tailored to meet your specific circumstances and objectives.

Topic Menu includes but is not limited to:

- The Hopeful Power of Negotiation.
- The Other Negotiator.
- The Art of Skilled Listening.
- Knowledge Is Power.
- Negotiating Creatively.
- Credibility and Rapport.
- Can You Negotiate When Trust Is Low?
- Building Leverage.
- STAR — CTIPS.
- Distributive Negotiation.
- Measuring Success and Walking Away.
- Hidden Factors That Shape Negotiation.
- Power of Preparation: "I FORESAW IT".
- Handling Sharp Tactics and Ethical Issues.
- Using Persuasion and Winning Buy-In.
- Managing Emotions and Psychological Traps.
- Negotiating with Godzilla and the Devil.
- Cross-Cultural Negotiation.
- Negotiating Work and the Workplace.
- Healing the Troubled Deal.
- Why the Trust Problem Is Fundamental.
- Confrontation and Negotiation.

How You Will Stand to Benefit as an Organisation

You will comprehend the art and science to negotiation and how to utilise the tools and tactics of successful engagement that affords the best possible opportunity of achieving your negotiating objectives. Business benefits as reported by previous course attendees include:

- Learning the critical task of understanding the other negotiator well; and the power of factual research, creative options, rapport, and hidden influences away from the negotiating table.
- How to wisely manage the task of dividing the pie, exploring what to strive for, how to make the first offer, and when to walk away.
- Understanding the critical challenge of solving the trust problem, which is present in most negotiations.
- How to achieve corporate goals through excellent negotiation techniques for the organisation's profit and benefit.
- How to see the value and the roadblocks in negotiations that may affect your organisation.

Who Benefits from this Course?

This course is specifically designed to take those responsible for leading negotiations and improve their strategies, thinking, tactics, techniques, and planning. People of varying skill levels up to and including CEOs and board members from many different industry verticals attend the course. Both the individuals and the companies sending them on the course experience the benefits of the training. This course is recommended for:

- Experienced Negotiators
- Sales and Business Development Staff
- Customer service and Care Personnel
- Senior Staff and Role Models
- Team Leaders & Supervisors
- Senior Management
- Executive Management
- Department Heads
- C-suite executives
- Board members
- Business owners

We customise- the course to every level and audience depending on your requirements.

How is this Course Delivered?

We fine-tune and customise this program for your organisation's training needs. You will save your organisation's time, resources and money by us coming to you and delivering the training at your premises or a location determined to be ideal for your needs and desired outcomes. The Business Negotiations Skills training course, based on your requirements, ranges from two to three days.

How many Delegates can Attend?

Typically, we suggest a maximum of 30 people from your organisation attend the training at any one time. This limit is suggested because of the *hands on* nature of the training and the individual feedback given to each person attending the training. Larger groups can be accommodated, however, and we can structure the training to best meet your requirements.

Management Training

Effective Communication Skills
Effective Business Communication Equals Greater Organisational Success

All programs are designed, written and produced to your organisation's specific requirements.

What You Will Learn

This course addresses communication techniques and strategies. It has been designed using critical information on how to use powerful, transformative communication skills to achieve successful outcomes. Participants will develop a deep understanding of the methodologies behind effective communication that produces positive organisational results. By understanding and implementing these concepts, businesspeople can stop making costly mistakes and improve existing opportunities.

Our first goal is awareness of how face-to-face talk works by comparing our common sense views of speaking with the basic models developed by communication researchers and theorists over the past 60 years. We investigate the essential processes that permit us to communicate — to understand and be understood by others — and discover that many of these methods are so profoundly learned that they operate automatically in most situations.

You will learn about the automatic and hidden processes that influence everyday talk, including our in-depth cultural learning and the non-conscious part of the mind, where much of this learning is stored. How they affect our conscious mind while we are in conversation with ourselves or another person. Moreover, you will come to understand that these processes do not operate independently of each other; they work through our sense of self. Instead of seeing the world the way it is, we see it the way we are. This course helps you be more conscious of these forces and to help you deal with them.

Every one of our training programs is uniquely designed and tailored to meet your specific circumstances and objectives.

Topic Menu includes but is not limited to:

- The Magic of Everyday Communication.
- Complex Layers of Face-to-Face Talk.
- The Social Context That Shapes Our Communication.
- The Cognitive Unconscious.
- The Conscious Mind in Communication.
- The Perception Factor.
- Emotion and Logic.
- Self-Esteem.
- Self-Talk and Self-Management.
- Challenges to Effective Communication.
- Talking to Build Relationships.
- Coping Mechanisms for Successful Communications.
- Differences, Disagreement, and Control.
- Commands, Accusations, and Blame.
- Assertive Dialogue to Manage Disagreement.
- Communication, Gender, and Culture.
- Visual, Auditory & Kinaesthetic.
- Social Style Theory.
- Next-Level Leadership-Communication.
- Appreciation and Productivity.
- Dialogue—Engaged Employees.
- Ethical Choices in Communication.
- Cialdini's Six Principles of Persuasion.
- Meta-Modelling.
- Critical Management & Common Sense.
- Writing Skills for Business Success.
- Presentation Skills That Work.

How You Will Stand to Benefit as an Organisation

In business we need to sustain relationships with others in order to get what we think we need and want from our work. To do this, we use a collection of behaviours described as communication skills. And, although we use them every day in our lives, we are often unaware of how they develop and function. This course provides a theoretical and practical survey of the ideas behind, and the practices of, effective communication. Business benefits as reported by previous course attendees include:

- Improved ethical communication skills makes you and your organisation more successful.
- We overview useful communication and learn to create and sustain relationships; control our automatic response to dealing with differences, disagreements, or disorder.
- You will learn that seeing what's real and right in front of us—and responding (communicating) accordingly—is not as easy as we think.
- How to achieve corporate goals through excellent communication techniques for the organisation's profit and benefit.
- The video sessions are incredibly informative. People can see how others see them, and also become aware of personal traits and idiosyncrasies that may negatively impact outcomes.

Who Benefits from this Course?

This course is for anyone in organisational life who wishes to improve their strategies and techniques in communicating positively. People of varying skill levels up to and including CEOs and board members from many different industry verticals attend the course. Both the individuals and the companies sending them on the course experience the benefits of the training. This course is recommended for:

- Sales and Business Development Staff
- Customer service and Care Personnel
- Senior Staff and Role Models
- Team Leaders & Supervisors
- Senior Management
- Executive Management
- Department Heads
- C-suite executives
- Board members
- Business owners

We customise- the course to every level and audience depending on your requirements.

How is this Course Delivered?

We fine-tune and customise this program for your organisation's training needs. You will save your organisation's time, resources and money by us coming to you and delivering the training at your premises or a location determined to be ideal for your needs and desired outcomes. The Effective Communication Skills training course, based on your requirements, ranges from two to three days.

How many Delegates can Attend?

Typically, we suggest a maximum of 24 people from your organisation attend the training at any one time. This number will need to be reduced if your organisation includes the video-recording assessment segment. Larger groups can be accommodated, however, and we can structure the training to best meet your requirements.

Management Training

Master Class: Critical Business Skills for Success

Learning the business execution techniques of stars like: Amazon, Apple, Nike & Starbucks

All programs are designed, written and produced to your organisation's specific requirements.

What You Will Learn

The world is full of great business ideas—products and service concepts that hold immense promise for businesses and the customers they serve. Still, what is the value of a great idea? It amounts to little if a business cannot execute? In this course, you will be exploring the ways in which successful firms like Amazon, Apple, Nike, Southwest, Starbucks, and others take great ideas from concept to reality by way of operational excellence. You will explore the fundamental aspects of operations that translate into winning techniques, covering such essential topics as supply management, distribution and logistics, and performance measurement.

You'll consider how companies can leverage both internal and external resources to extend their reach in the market and ensure profitability. In today's hyper-competitive market environment, organisations are seeking to implement processes that create the highest value for the business and its customers. Throughout this Master Class, you will explore how organisations of all kinds can achieve optimal outcomes through implementation of management methods based on lean thinking. You will also see that operations are instrumental as a value generator and competitive differentiator in every business, ensuring that the right products and services are available in the right form and quantity at the right place and time—and at a competitive price. You will come to realise during the course that operations management touches virtually every facet of our everyday existence and ensures our quality of life.

The course covers the area of *facts and figures*, which show how effectively any organisation is fulfilling its strategic mission and operating objectives by providing critical financial information. You will learn more about ratio analysis, a useful tool that allows us to use financial statements to evaluate an organisation's profitability, efficiency, liquidity, and risk, while allowing comparisons to other organisations, including competitors. You also discuss the breakeven analysis, rick/return, and more.

You will explore such topics as career success and survival, the critical nature of leadership, the importance of great interpersonal skills and emotional intelligence, and effective communication with co-workers and employees. You will work on marketing strategy and marketing tactics. These topics include products and services, branding, pricing, and communications, including advertising, social media, and word of mouth. Marketing done well is the basis on which companies grow, innovate, and fend off competition. The course is designed to provide you with the tools you need to understand marketing and make sound marketing decisions.

Every one of our training programs is uniquely designed and tailored to meet your specific circumstances and objectives.

Topic Menu includes but is not limited to:

- *Strategy*: Strategy is making choices.
- *Strategy*: How Apple raises competitive barriers.
- *Strategy*: The danger of straddling.
- *Strategy*: What Trader Joe's doesn't do.
- *Strategy*: First Movers versus Fast Followers.
- *Strategy*: Netflix and Blockbuster.
- *Strategy*: Anticipating your rival's response.
- *Strategy*: Why did Disney buy Pixar?
- *Strategy*: The Diversification Discount.
- *Strategy*: Forward and Backward integration.
- *Strategy*: The Winner's Curse of Mergers and Acquisitions.
- *Strategy*: Launching a lean start-up.
- *Operations*: The Power of Superior Operations.
- *Operations*: Leaner, Meaner Production.
- *Operations*: Refining service operations.
- *Operations*: Matching supply and demand.
- *Operations*: Managing supply and suppliers.
- *Operations*: The long reach of logistics.
- *Operations*: Rethinking your business processes.
- *Operations*: Measuring operational performance.
- *Operations*: Keeping an eye on your margins.
- *Operations*: Leveraging your supply chain.
- *Operations*: Reducing risk and building resilience.
- *Accounting & Finance*: Accounting and financial decision-making tools.
- *Accounting & Finance*: Ratio Analyses.
- *Accounting & Finance*: Understanding the time value of money.
- *Accounting & Finance*: The trade-off between risk and return.
- *Accounting & Finance*: Weighing the costs of debt and equity.
- *Organisational Behaviour*: Achieving results in your organisation.
- *Organisational Behaviour*: The value of great leadership.
- *Organisational Behaviour*: Emotional Intelligence in the workplace.
- *Organisational Behaviour*: The Art of Effective Communications.
- *Organisational Behaviour*: Motivation-Performance Connection.
- *Organisational Behaviour*: Winning with teamwork.
- *Organisational Behaviour*: Coaching — From the rugby field to the boardroom.
- *Organisational Behaviour*: Understanding Power Relationships.
- *Organisational Behaviour*: Handling Workplace Conflict.
- *Organisational Behaviour*: Ethics and the Bathsheba Syndrome.
- *Organisational Behaviour*: Leading real organisational change.
- *Organisational Behaviour*: Lifelong learning for career success.
- *Marketing*: What is marketing?
- *Marketing*: How to segment a market.
- *Marketing*: Targeting a Market Segment.
- *Marketing*: Positioning your offering.
- *Marketing*: Identifying sources of sales growth.
- *Marketing*: Deriving value from your customers.
- *Marketing*: Creating great customer experiences.
- *Marketing*: The tactics of successful branding.
- *Marketing*: Customer-Focused Pricing.
- *Marketing*: Marketing communications that work.
- *Marketing*: The promise and perils of social media.
- *Marketing*: Innovative marketing research techniques.

How You Will Stand to Benefit as an Organisation

This comprehensive Master Class is a rich and dynamic program that encompasses: strategy, operations, finance and accounting, organisational behaviour, and marketing. All the tools and resources necessary for managers and leaders to take decisive and prudent action that will you're your organisation with the best possible opportunity of achieving sensational results.

- This course is a multifaceted one, analysing how an organisation's proclivity for control and its appetite for flexibility can catapult outcomes from good to great.
- Nobody tells you how demanding management is when you're offered a promotion or a role; this course provides you with the tools and confidence to implement excellent strategies and tactics to achieve impressive and lasting organisational results that will make you proud.
- Understanding the principles of strategic thinking, operations management, finance and accounting, organisational behaviour, and marketing guarantees you are a well-equipped and knowledgeable leader that your people will want to follow.
- How to achieve corporate goals through understanding not to fear the future but harness its potential for the organisation's benefit.
- By understanding more about the diverse components of an organisation you become a more valuable manager that delivers value while driving results.

Who Benefits from this Course?

This course is specifically designed to take leaders and accomplished managers and improve their thinking and understanding of five core components applicable in any oganisation. People of varying skill levels up to and including CEOs and board members from many different industry verticals attend the course. This course is recommended for:

- New managers
- Experienced Managers taking on new responsibilities
- Human Resources Personnel
- Senior Staff and Role Models
- Team Leaders & Supervisors
- Senior Management
- Executive Management
- Department Heads
- C-suite executives
- Board members
- Business owners

We customise- the course to every level and audience depending on your requirements.

How is this Course Delivered?

After an initial consultation with your organisation, you will decide the areas of focus and the relevant sub-topics that align with the objectives, goals, and the desired business results you need. We then customise the training. You will save your organisation's time, resources and money by us coming to you and delivering the training at your premises or a location determined to be ideal for your needs and desired outcomes. The Critical Business Skills Master Class, based on your requirements, ranges from three to seven days.

How many Delegates can Attend?

Typically, we suggest a maximum of 30 people from your organisation attend the training at any one time. This limit is suggested because of the *hands on* nature of the training and the group feedback given. Larger groups can be accommodated, however, and we can structure the training to best meet your requirements.

Triskaidekaphobia strategy

Ric Willmot

It's just bad luck that the 13th is so often on a Friday. But even the triskaidekaphobics eschewed their fears to celebrate the retirement on Friday 13th July of an executive director of Toll who had been 53 years in the transport industry and 50 years with the one company.

It was a celebration of a career, a reunion of retired colleagues, a toast by peers, and a fond farewell to a unique employee. In an era when diversity of roles, multitudes of experiences, and a resume of varied employers are sought after in new hires, we listened to stalwarts of an industry praise the longevity and loyalty of a 50-year company man who had risen from the ranks of truck driver to senior management.

Whilst famous triskaidekaphobes like Napoleon and Franklin Roosevelt would appreciate the loyalty of a long-term company man, CEOs are struggling with Generation Y, who are always looking for their next opportunity brightly shining on the horizon. Recruitment firms proclaim that the multitude of companies and careers add value to the resume and make the candidate more attractive by adding to the organisation's knowledge bank.

These are opposing perspectives on employee value, neither right nor wrong, one not better than the other, just different. The same is true of strategy. There is no one right way to develop strategy and there is no one right way to lead an organisation to success. There are, I believe, guiding principles to consider.

Three things we need to be successful in business:
1. Market need
2. Competency
3. Passion

Market need comes in three flavours:

1. Pre-existing need – the need has always been around, it is still here today and will continue into the future. Examples include such segments as food, clothing and housing.
2. Created need – the need that gets created by entrepreneurs who can generate market desire by exceptional marketing based upon the perceived need. None of us needed a Walkman until the chairman of Sony instructed his engineers to build one. The iPod is simply the latest iteration, albeit a very technologically good one. This is called innovation. Nobody needed a cash register, but shopkeepers did need to track sales and cash transactions.
3. Anticipated need – the anticipated solutions to needs not yet born, but likely to take life.

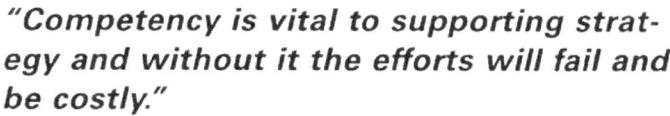

Competency is vital to supporting strategy and without it the efforts will fail and be costly. But not only must you have the competency required to support your strategy in going to market, potential customers must also perceive you as being competent. We wouldn't have much faith in a dentist with bad teeth, a poorly dressed financial adviser or an obese dietician.

And you must be passionate about what your business provides. Richard Branson is undoubtedly passionate, and Steve Irwin was the epitome of passion for his wildlife message.

It is at the confluence of these three guiding principles where your strategic success is at its best. If you have competency and passion but no market need then you may have a wonderful product, service or message – it's just that no one wants it. If you have market need and passion but no competency, then you will lose out to your competitors every time. And if you have market need and competency but no passion, you will never enthuse the market place and they will fail to show up. Because, metaphorically, so have you.

The needs of the transport industry have changed over the last 53 years. Some needs have always been there, like moving freight from point to point. Other needs were created, such as overnight express, whilst anticipating the desire for refrigerated transport of fresh foods intra- and inter-state gave rise to players in that industry.

Brian continually acquired new skills and then applied them to purpose at work. Else how might he have ever been promoted from a truck driver to executive director? And there certainly was passion, for the industry, for his employer of 50 years, and for the people in his life.

Successful business strategy is to understand and embrace the driving, compelling force that will bring the opportunities of your marketplace to your door. Treat yourself and your customers well, strive for success but don't get hung up on perfection, and keep your eye on the horizon for what might motivate you next.

Gen Y are proud of their diversity of roles. This 71 year old 'company man' was more ebullient, insightful, and interesting than most double-degree MBA executives I meet. Strategic success is not an event but a way of being, continually evolving and seeking that next new opportunity to build and grow upon the past. Life, just like strategy, is about being active, being involved and being vibrant.

Apollo 13 launched from Pad 39 at 13:13 local time, only to be struck by an explosion on April 13. James Lovell piloted the Lunar Module Aquarius safely into the Pacific Ocean near Samoa using carefully considered strategies. No doubt our Friday 13th-retired company man will be splashing around in the Pacific Ocean near Palm Beach very soon too.

Ric Willmot, known as 'The Consultant's Consultant,' is the CEO of Executive Wisdom Consulting Group (www.executivewisdom.com), and the founder of the Society for Executive Wisdom (www.executivewisdomsociety.com).

Management Thinking Skills Training

Argumentation
A Guide to Effective Reasoning and its Role in Organisations and Management

All programs are designed, written and produced to your organisation's specific requirements.

What You Will Learn

Argumentation is not a very well understood aspect of human communication. Far from the connotations of being combative, contentious, unpleasant and quarrelsome, argumentation is the study of reasons given by people to justify their acts or beliefs and to influence the thought or action of others. It's about influence and persuasion through communication that attempts to motivate and persuade others through reasoned judgment. The course is introductory in that it does not presume any prior study of argumentation. Because argumentation is a daily occurrence–everyone does it–the course is also sophisticated in that it offers a systematic analysis, a precise vocabulary, and a philosophical foundation for what all too often is an activity that we conduct intuitively and unconsciously.

We discuss the differences between formal and informal reasoning. The main patterns of formal deduction—categorical, conditional, and disjunctive reasoning—are described in the training. You will examine aspects of argumentation strategies and tactics, as it applies to an organisational setting. The course defines the components of an argument (a claim, evidence, an inference linking the evidence to the claim, and a warrant authorising the inference) and describes how these components can be represented diagrammatically. During the training course you will move from simple arguments to examine the structure of more complex arguments. Multiple, coordinative, and subordinative structures illustrate the patterns by which parts of complex arguments are brought together. You will explore how the choices among these patterns make a difference to the understanding of the overall argument.

Every one of our training programs is uniquely designed and tailored to meet your specific circumstances and objectives.

Topic Menu includes but is not limited to:

- Argumentation and Rhetoric.
- Primary Assumptions of Argumentation.
- Formal and Informal Argumentation.
- Argument Analysis and Diagramming.
- Complex Structures of Argument.
- Our constructed reality.
- Case Construction—Requirements and Options.
- Stasis—The Heart of the Controversy.
- Attack and Defence.
- Language and Style in Argument.
- Evaluating Evidence.
- Reasoning from Parts to Whole.
- Reasoning with Comparisons.
- Establishing Correlations.
- Moving from Cause to Effect.
- Hybrid Patterns of Inference.
- Validity and Fallacies.
- Arguments among Experts.

How You Will Stand to Benefit as an Organisation

The skills taught in this course will provide the necessary intellectual background to argumentation. It is necessary to understand rhetoric and logic in their classical context because these terms either have acquired negative stereotypes in contemporary culture or they have fallen into disuse. This training program will help you understand the technique of argumentation and by understanding the classic meaning and structure it will enable you to implement effective reasoning more successfully. You will then achieve greater influence, status, and success in your role. Learning benefits as reported by previous course attendees include:

- This course explores the importance of an audience, the regulation of uncertainty, the difference between justification and proof, the cooperative nature of the enterprise, and the acceptance of risk.
- The program provides a comprehensive understanding what it means to argue as a means of reaching decisions.
- Understanding how controversies arise and how the most basic element of argument is the claim.
- How to map your case for reasoning — your set of arguments that you bring forward to support or oppose a claim.
- Understanding that identifying issues in a specific case, and addressing the issues meets the initial burden of proof. Making your argument and reasoning more compelling.

Who Benefits from this Course?

This course is appropriate for anyone in business or government. People necessarily make decisions and are called on to solve problems every day. It is a foundation and cornerstone course that all organisations should have as a "must-do" professional development learning program. Both the individuals and the companies sending them on the course experience the benefits of the training. This course is recommended for:

- New Managers
- Experienced Managers taking on new responsibilities
- HR personnel
- Senior Staff and Role Models
- Team Leaders & Supervisors
- Middle Management
- Executive Management
- Senior Managers & Department Heads
- C-suite executives
- Board members
- Business owner

We customise- the course to every level and audience depending on your requirements.

How is this Course Delivered?

We fine-tune and customise this program for your organisation's training needs. You will save your organisation's time, resources and money by us coming to you and delivering the training at your premises or a location determined to be ideal for your needs and desired outcomes. The Argumentation training course, is usually delivered in one day.

How many Delegates can Attend?

Typically, we suggest a maximum of 40 people from your organisation attend the training at any one time. This is a highly engaging and interactive training program. Larger groups can be accommodated, however, and we can structure the training to best meet your requirements.

Management Thinking Skills Training

Creative Thinking Skills
The Creative Thinker's Toolkit for Transformative Leaders & Managers

All programs are designed, written and produced to your organisation's specific requirements.

What You Will Learn

The highest level of human thought is creativity. Rather than being a skill that is exclusive to a rare gifted few, it is a way of thinking and behaving that can be achieved by all. However, many see creativity as mysterious, intuitive, or strictly innate. To the contrary, creative thinking is a skill that can be examined, practised, and deliberately developed. In this course you study the approaches, and tools that are most effective in moving creativity from a chance occurrence to a more predictable outcome.

Throughout this course you make direct connections between deliberate creative methods used by great creators such as Mozart, Spielberg, Picasso, Jobs, Wright, Edison and learnable tools that can be applied to a range of creative challenges. This course also examines how creativity is a natural human phenomenon, drawing on information from evolution that highlights the fact that our ability to creatively solve problems provides the human species with a crucial competitive advantage.

The course also studies the ability to think in lateral ways, being flexible in thought as opposed to vertical thinking, which is digging deeper into the same line of reasoning is essential to the generation of breakthrough ideas. This program introduces the complete creative process and explores how individuals report different degrees of preference for the thinking associated with the four areas found in the universal creative process: clarify, ideate, develop, and implement. The teaching moves you sequentially through the stages of the creative process, adding a large set of tools designed to improve problem clarification, idea generation, solution development, and implementation planning.

Every one of our training programs is uniquely designed and tailored to meet your specific circumstances and objectives.

Topic Menu includes but is not limited to:

- The Creative Person — Practice and Passion.
- Lateral thinking is a survival skill.
- Creative Styles—Adapters & Innovators.
- Combining opposites — Diverge, then converge.
- Principles for unleashing your imagination.
- Principles for converging on the best ideas.
- Clarifying the challenge.
- Classic brainstorming and brain-writing.
- Tools for enhanced brainstorming.
- Borrowing and modifying ideas.
- Systematic tools to generate new ideas.
- Developing ideas – Techniques toward great solutions.
- Evaluating creative solutions and making decisions.
- The persuasion and selling of new ideas.
- Creative Leadership – Regardless of your role.
- Overcoming roadblocks and barriers.
- Living a creative life.

How You Will Stand to Benefit as an Organisation

You will comprehend how to utilise the tools of analysis and tactics of creative thinking to implement action that affords the best possible opportunity of achieving your organisation's objectives. Business benefits as reported by previous course attendees include:

- Explore what it means to be a creative person.
- The effective balance between divergent thinking and convergent thinking is the heartbeat of the creative process.
- Creativity involves both the head and the heart.
- Life is fraught with challenges, and thus, many consider creative thinking to be a life skill. As such, how you can apply the material from this course is limited only by your imagination.

Who Benefits from this Course?

This course is for any organisation who wishes its staff to improve their creative thinking skills. People of varying skill levels up to and including CEOs and board members from many different industry verticals attend the course. Both the individuals and the companies sending them on the course experience the benefits of the training. This course is recommended for:

- Research and Development Personnel
- Marketing and Business Development
- Sales and Customer Service Personnel
- Human Resources
- Experienced Managers taking on new responsibilities
- Senior Staff and Role Models
- Team Leaders & Supervisors
- Senior Management
- Executive Management
- Department Heads
- C-suite executives
- Board members
- Business owners

We customise- the course to every level and audience depending on your requirements.

How is this Course Delivered?

We fine-tune and customise this program for your organisation's training needs. You will save your organisation's time, resources and money by us coming to you and delivering the training at your premises or a location determined to be ideal for your needs and desired outcomes. The Creative Thinking Skills training course, is nearly always best delivered in two days. It can be truncated to a one-day program if required, but this requires, obviously, some content to be removed.

How many Delegates can Attend?

Typically, we suggest a maximum of 40 people from your organisation attend the training at any one time. This is a highly engaging and interactive training program. Larger groups can be accommodated, however, and we can structure the training to best meet your requirements.

"Ric is an expert in Change Management and Organizational Development. I have had the opportunity to engage Ric as a training consultant for several training programmes in Malaysia, attended by senior executives and c-suites from different countries. He could always be counted on to deliver excellent executive-level training programmes. He is highly interactive in conducting training, and he never fails to inspire the audience. Ric is very professional and supportive; it was such a great pleasure working with him. I have no hesitation in recommending Ric, and I look forward to working with him again!"

— **Jazlyn Lee, Sunway University, Malaysia**

Management Thinking Skills Training

Critical Thinking Skills

A Scientific Guide to Critical Thinking and the Role of Your Deceptive Mind

All programs are designed, written and produced to your organisation's specific requirements.

What You Will Learn

In this course, you will learn the many ways in which our human brains deceive us and lead us to conclusions that have little to do with reality. That's a very big problem when making crucial business decisions. You will learn strategies that can be used to combat the mind's many deceptions and have you making better, smarter, and more appropriate business decisions. We rely on our memories as if they were accurate recordings of the past, but the evidence shows that we should be highly suspicious of even the most vivid and confident memories. Additionally, a host of logical flaws and cognitive biases plague our thinking. In this course, you will explore logical errors and cognitive biases in detail, learning how they affect business thinking in often subtle ways.

We discuss how you can accurately use critical thinking skills and tools to combat the deceptions of your mind. You will learn how to apply critical thinking, knowledge of science, and knowledge of the mechanisms of self-deception to everyday practice. By the end of the course, you will have a thorough understanding of what constitutes critical thinking and why we all so desperately need it in business. The philosophy and practice of critical thinking and science are the tools that everyone in organisational life needs to be a better problem-solver and decision-maker. This course is a must-do program for anyone and everyone who has responsibilities for "thinking" at work.

Every one of our training programs is uniquely designed and tailored to meet your specific circumstances and objectives.

Topic Menu includes but is not limited to:

- Thinking about Thinking.
- The Neuroscience of Belief.
- Errors of Perception.
- Flaws and Fabrications of Memory.
- Pattern Recognition—Seeing what's not there.
- Our constructed reality.
- The structure and purpose of Argumentation.
- Logic and logical fallacies.
- Cognitive Biases.
- Toward better estimates of what's probable.
- Culture and mass delusions.
- Philosophy and presuppositions of science.
- Science and the supernatural.
- Great scientific blunders.
- Science versus pseudoscience.
- The many kinds of pseudoscience.
- The trap of grand conspiracy thinking.
- Denialism—Rejecting science and history.
- Marketing, scams, and urban legends.
- Science, media, and democracy.
- Experts and consensus.

How You Will Stand to Benefit as an Organisation

The skills taught in this course will help you operate on the metacognitive level so that you can think about the process of your thinking. The human brain is the universal tool by which we understand ourselves and the universe in which we live. By understanding the nature of human cognition and the methods of thinking clearly and critically, we can avoid common errors and make the best use of our minds. Learning benefits as reported by previous course attendees include:

- This course explores what is called metacognition: thinking about thinking itself.
- Understanding how everything we think we see, hear, and experience is not a direct recording of the outside world; instead, it is a construction.
- Understanding that information is filtered, distorted, compared, and confabulated—ultimately to be woven into a narrative that fits our assumptions about the business decisions we make.
- How our brains have other interesting strengths and weaknesses that can further inform our thinking, like how we are generally very good at pattern recognition.
- Understanding that many of us are inherently poor at probability and statistics, and this innumeracy opens us up to deception and errors in thinking.
- Perhaps our greatest weakness is our susceptibility to delusion, the ability to hold a false belief against all evidence.

Who Benefits from this Course?

This course is appropriate for anyone in business or government. People necessarily make decisions and are called on to solve problems every day. It is a foundation and cornerstone course that all organisations should have as a "must-do" professional development learning program. Both the individuals and the companies sending them on the course experience the benefits of the training. This course is recommended for:

- New Managers
- Experienced Managers taking on new responsibilities
- HR personnel
- Senior Staff and Role Models
- Team Leaders & Supervisors
- Middle Management
- Executive Management
- Senior Managers & Department Heads
- C-suite executives
- Board members
- Business owner

We customise- the course to every level and audience depending on your requirements.

How is this Course Delivered?

We fine-tune and customise this program for your organisation's training needs. You will save your organisation's time, resources and money by us coming to you and delivering the training at your premises or a location determined to be ideal for your needs and desired outcomes. The Critical Thinking Skills training course, is nearly always best delivered in two days. It can be truncated to a one-day program if required, but this requires, obviously, some content to be removed.

How many Delegates can Attend?

Typically, we suggest a maximum of 40 people from your organisation attend the training at any one time. This is a highly engaging and interactive training program. Larger groups can be accommodated, however, and we can structure the training to best meet your requirements

Management Thinking Skills Training

Building Brain Fitness
How to Optimise Your Brain's Power

All programs are designed, written and produced to your organisation's specific requirements.

What You Will Learn

You can increase the power of your brain through your effort. Your brain's ability to change in response to experience—called plasticity—is the key to understanding your mind's development. The good news is that no matter how old you are, you can still take an active part in influencing brain plasticity. The brain is dependent on your experiences and continues to evolve throughout your life.

If you wish to improve your brainpower, it's necessary to understand how it works. In this course, you will learn how the brain is organised, how it develops, and how messages are transmitted through the brain's electrochemical pathways. Neuroscientists like to say that "cells that fire together wire together." Think of brain circuits like friendships: Those that are maintained and enriched will endure, while those that are neglected disappear. The course also studies how intelligence is not something like eye colour that you're born with and cannot change—it is a dynamic process that can be favourably influenced by choices you make. You will learn that attention—also referred to as focus and concentration—must be rock solid in order to marshal the effort needed to improve your brain's performance.

You will learn that if any piece of information can be instantly retrieved via a Google search, then why bother to remember it? Because the act of remembering something facilitates the activation and retention of circuits within the brain that contribute to the brain's optimal functioning. Over-reliance on electronic information aids can result in a disuse atrophy of your memory powers, but this atrophy can be overcome by deliberate efforts to improve memory. Deliberate practice is the key to improving performance and creativity in all areas of human endeavour, including work and play.

By challenging your brain to learn new information throughout your life, you build up cognitive reserve. The more you have accumulated over your lifetime, the less susceptible you will be to deficits in your later years. In general, the more education and knowledge people acquire over their lifetime, the less likely they are in their later years to be diagnosed with dementia. In this practical course, you'll learn what steps you can take in your own life to enhance your brain function.

Every one of our training programs is uniquely designed and tailored to meet your specific circumstances and objectives.

Topic Menu includes but is not limited to:

- How Your Brain Works.
- How Your Brain Changes.
- Creativity and the Playful Brain.
- Focusing Your Attention.
- Enhancing Your Memory.
- Exercising Your Working Memory.
- Putting Your Senses to Work.
- Enlisting Your Emotional Memory.
- Practicing for Peak Performance.
- Taking Advantage of Technology.
- Building Your Cognitive Reserve.

How You Will Stand to Benefit as an Organisation

You will comprehend how to utilise the tools of building and optimising mental fitness and strength. Business benefits as reported by previous course attendees include:

- At every moment, your activities and your thoughts are modifying your brain.
- Enriched health and well-being leads to intelligence improvements.
- Just as an athlete cannot perform optimally without endurance, you cannot expect to achieve a superpower brain without being able to laser focus your mental energies.
- You'll learn how to enlist all of your senses in exercises and techniques that can enhance brain function in visual imagery, imagination, and long-term memory.

Who Benefits from this Course?

This course is for any organisation who wishes its staff to improve their creative thinking skills. People of varying skill levels up to and including CEOs and board members from many different industry verticals attend the course. Both the individuals and the companies sending them on the course experience the benefits of the training. This course is recommended for:

- Research and Development Personnel
- Marketing and Business Development
- Sales and Customer Service Personnel
- Human Resources
- Experienced Managers taking on new responsibilities
- Senior Staff and Role Models
- Team Leaders & Supervisors
- Senior Management
- Executive Management
- Department Heads
- C-suite executives
- Board members
- Business owners

We customise- the course to every level and audience depending on your requirements.

How is this Course Delivered?

We fine-tune and customise this program for your organisation's training needs. You will save your organisation's time, resources and money by us coming to you and delivering the training at your premises or a location determined to be ideal for your needs and desired outcomes. The Building Brain Fitness training course, is best delivered as a one day program. It can be extended to a two-day program if required, by including some specialised and worthwhile exercises, challenges, case studies, and more.

How many Delegates can Attend?

Typically, we suggest a maximum of 40 people from your organisation attend the training at any one time. This is a highly engaging and interactive training program. Larger groups can be accommodated, however, and we can structure the training to best meet your requirements.

"*I have worked with Ric Willmot on numerous occasions for events in the APAC/MEA region. I can confidently say that Ric is the most well prepared, highly knowledgeable and professional trainer I have ever had the privilege of working with. Training programs conducted by Ric were very well received by the attendees who were mainly at senior management level. In fact, promoting events became that much easier and highly profitable because of Ric's involvement as the course trainer. With Ric, it's all about nurturing relationships and sharing knowledge. I am extremely eager to work with him again in the near future!*"
— **Pervinder Singh, EU-Malaysia Chamber of Commerce and Industry**

Management Thinking Skills Training
Psychology of Influence
Creating a High Performance Organisation

All programs are designed, written and produced to your organisation's specific requirements.

What You Will Learn

What makes working in organisations an interesting, and at times, a challenging proposition is the fact that enterprises are made up of human beings. Each has their unique personality, talents, motives, communication styles, and personal idiosyncrasies that can make the work environment pleasant or unbearable.

In this highly engaging workshop, you will learn why power is a necessary element for organisational work. Ric will share his experience and make you understand the machinations of the sources of power in organisations. Power in organisations has three sources:

- Position: Your rank in the organisation confers some level of formal power.
- Relationships: Informal power stems from your relationship with others.
- Personal: Some people generate from within; that power is based on general knowledge, technical competency, and an ability to articulate ideas or vision for others to follow.

To create a high-performance organisation, Ric will facilitate this workshop for you to increase your power — power you can wield to achieve goals, large and small. If you want to learn real-world managerial influence and persuasion, not just textbook theory, this training course is the answer for you and your organisation. If you desire to understand what happens in the most favourable people-driven organisations around the world, in the boardrooms and executive suites, and on the front line where the workers have to make it happen; this program will allow you to learn what you need to know.

Every one of our training programs is uniquely designed and tailored to meet your specific circumstances and objectives.

Topic Menu includes but is not limited to:

- The principles of positive persuasion.
- Understanding what is stopping you from being successful.
- How to be a positive power manager.
- Why personality profiling tests and psychometrics aren't working, and what you can do about it now.
- Ways to perform evaluation and provide feedback to improve performance.
- Communicating in difficult situations.
- Understanding power relationships.
- Developing an agile and dynamic brain.
- Ways to focus your attention during critical moments.
- Work backwards to ensure completeness of thought.
- Cultivate consistent performance-thinking.
- Meta-Modelling, and other tools.
- Assertiveness and responsiveness.
- Preferences in processing and communicating.
- Handling workplace conflict.
- Coaching at work and managing people.

How You Will Stand to Benefit as an Organisation

You will comprehend why people behave the way they do at work and identify the recognisable pattern of human behaviour within organisation. Benefits as reported by previous course attendees include:

- Discover what leaders and professionals can and should do to bring out the very best in their people at work.
- Learn the critical concepts and strategies to maximise the performance and job satisfaction for all employees to make the organisation successful.
- Explore the critical nature of communication and leadership to create people power at work and a culture that maximises human performance.
- You'll learn the concept of behavioural economics and its impact on organisations.
- You will recognise the psychological factors of your environment and how it affects the group dynamics. If conflict arises, you will learn how to decipher and resolve the conflict at work.

Who Benefits from this Course?

This course is for any organisation who wishes its staff to improve their creative thinking skills. People of varying skill levels up to and including CEOs and board members from many different industry verticals attend the course. Both the individuals and the companies sending them on the course experience the benefits of the training. This course is recommended for:

- Research and Development Personnel
- Marketing and Business Development
- Sales and Customer Service Personnel
- Human Resources
- Experienced Managers taking on new responsibilities
- Senior Staff and Role Models
- Team Leaders & Supervisors
- Senior Management
- Executive Management
- Department Heads
- C-suite executives
- Board members
- Business owners

We customise- the course to every level and audience depending on your requirements.

How is this Course Delivered?

We fine-tune and customise this program for your organisation's training needs. You will save your organisation's time, resources and money by us coming to you and delivering the training at your premises or a location determined to be ideal for your needs and desired outcomes. The Psychology of Influence training course, is best delivered as a two or three day program.

How many Delegates can Attend?

Typically, we suggest a maximum of 40 people from your organisation attend the training at any one time. This is a highly engaging and interactive training program. Larger groups can be accommodated, however, and we can structure the training to best meet your requirements.

Management Thinking Skills Training

Scepticism as a Business Tool
How Management can Think Like a Scientist

All programs are designed, written and produced to your organisation's specific requirements.

What You Will Learn

A 2006 Reader's Digest survey of 1,006 adult Britons reported that 43% said they could read other people's thoughts or have their thoughts read. 26% said they had sensed when a loved-one was ill or in trouble. And 62% said that they could tell who was calling before they picked up the phone. A fifth said that they had seen a ghost, and nearly a third said that they believed that near-death experiences are evidence for an afterlife. The National Science Foundation (NSF) concluded: "Such beliefs may sometimes be fuelled by the media's miscommunication of science and the scientific process."

Part of the problem may be that 70% of people still do not understand the scientific process, defined as grasping probability, the experimental method, and hypothesis testing. This being true, it poses questions about the vulnerability of thinking in business. How well can we make decisions in business when these types of survey results are so worrying? One solution, then, is to teach how science works to help us be more scientific in business thinking.

Belief systems are powerful, pervasive, and enduring. This course synthesises 30 years of research to answer the questions of how and why we believe what we do in all aspects of our lives. In this course, we are interested in understanding not just why people believe weird things but why people believe anything at all. We form our beliefs for a variety of subjective, personal, emotional, and psychological reasons in the context of environments created by family, friends, colleagues, culture, and society at large. After forming our beliefs, we then defend, justify, and rationalise them with a host of intellectual reasons, cogent arguments, and rational explanations.

This course will teach you how to reason like a scientist to give you the necessary tools for evaluating claims and determining whether or not a belief you hold is provisionally true, likely false, or in between.

Every one of our training programs is uniquely designed and tailored to meet your specific circumstances and objectives.

Topic Menu includes but is not limited to:

- The Virtues of Scepticism.
- Scepticism and Science.
- Mistakes in Thinking We All Make.
- Cognitive Biases and Their Effects.
- Wrong Thinking in Everyday Life.
- The Neuroscience of Belief.
- The Paranormal and the Supernatural.
- Science versus Pseudoscience.
- Comparing SETI and UFOlogy.
- Science, History, and Pseudohistory.
- The Lure of Conspiracy Theories.
- Inside the Modern Cult.
- Your Sceptical Toolkit.
- Detective Columbo.
- Creative Leadership – Regardless of your role.
- Overcoming roadblocks and barriers.
- Living a creative life.

How You Will Stand to Benefit as an Organisation

The thesis of the course is straightforward: You will comprehend how to think like a scientist so that you may bring greater clarity to your business and management thinking. Thereby producing better business decisions. Business benefits as reported by previous course attendees include:

- Explore what it means to be a scientific thinker and how it can be transferred over to organisational life and decision-making.
- The effective balance between fact-only thinking and intuition.
- Understanding that the brain is a belief engine. Once beliefs are formed, the brain begins to look for and find confirming evidence in support of those beliefs.
- This course will teach you how to think and reason like a scientist to give you the necessary tools for evaluating claims and determining whether or not a belief you hold is provisionally true.
- You will learn that beliefs come first; explanations for beliefs follow. This process belief-dependent realism, where our perceptions about reality are dependent on the beliefs that we hold about it can be the cause of poor or flawed business decisions.

Who Benefits from this Course?

This course is for any organisation who wants its people to improve their fact-based thinking skills. People of varying skill levels up to and including CEOs and board members from many different industry verticals attend the course. Both the individuals and the companies sending them on the course experience the benefits of the training. This course is recommended for:

- Research and Development Personnel
- Marketing and Business Development
- Sales and Customer Service Personnel
- Human Resources
- Experienced Managers taking on new responsibilities
- Senior Staff and Role Models
- Team Leaders & Supervisors
- Senior Management
- Executive Management
- Department Heads
- C-suite executives
- Board members
- Business owners

We customise- the course to every level and audience depending on your requirements.

How is this Course Delivered?

We fine-tune and customise this program for your organisation's training needs. You will save your organisation's time, resources and money by us coming to you and delivering the training at your premises or a location determined to be ideal for your needs and desired outcomes. The Scepticism as a Business Tool training course, is nearly always best delivered in two days. It can be truncated to a one-day program if required, but this requires, obviously, some content to be removed.

How many Delegates can Attend?

Typically, we suggest a maximum of 30 people from your organisation attend the training at any one time. This is a highly engaging and interactive training program. Larger groups can be accommodated, however, and we can structure the training to best meet your requirements.

Management Thinking Skills Training

The Hidden Factor
Thinking Differently to Achieve Organisational Success

All programs are designed, written and produced to your organisation's specific requirements.

What You Will Learn

In this course, you will explore the pragmatic benefits of diversity. You will see how differences in how people think contribute to collective performance in a variety of contexts, including how differences improve prediction and problem solving and how they make systems more robust.

The ideas in this course have the potential to transform how you think, live, and work and how people contribute to success in any group, team, department, organisation. You will discover that your potential to contribute depends on building tools that complement the skills of others, and you will find that a focus on individual achievement can be self-defeating.

Optimal teams, groups, and organisations require diverse talent. To perform well, these teams, groups, and organisations must promote diverse ways of thinking. Diversity is linked to innovation and economic growth because continued growth depends on new perspectives and on recombining new ideas. Organisations that do not promote diversity fail. You will learn how cognitive difference plus cognitive depth allows groups to make better forecasts, find more innovative solutions to problems, and adapt to challenges.

In this course, you will encounter topics such as groupthink and crowdsourcing, and you will learn how to make sound predictions using a variety of methods. This course will forever change how you think of diversity: You will no longer think of diversity in political or identity terms; instead, you will see diversity as central to understanding, progress, and robustness.

Every one of our training programs is uniquely designed and tailored to meet your specific circumstances and objectives.

Topic Menu includes but is not limited to:

- Why Now? The Rise of Diversity.
- Diversity Squared.
- The Wisdom of Crowds.
- The Diversity Prediction Theorem Times Three.
- Foxes and Hedgehogs—Can You Really Be Diverse?
- Estimating and Predicting.
- Problem Solving.
- Diverse Perspectives.
- Diversity Trumps Ability.
- Beware of False Prophets—No Free Lunch.
- Experimentation, Variation, and Six Sigma.
- Diversity and Robustness.
- Inescapable Benefits of Diversity.
- Homophily, Incentives, and Groupthink.
- The Problem of Diverse Preferences.
- The Team. The Team. The Team.

How You Will Stand to Benefit as an Organisation

The thesis of the course is straightforward: You will comprehend how diverse thinking brings greater opportunities to your organisation through improved business and management thinking. Business benefits as reported by previous course attendees include:

- An unwillingness to challenge status-quo thinking can be fatal.
- You will learn how the lessons and insights of diversity have become even more relevant in an increasingly flat, complex world in which challenges and opportunities change quickly.
- Understanding that long-term success requires continued growth and the addition of new tools such as diversity thinking, problem-solving, and decision-making.
- This course will teach you how the rules that have worked in the past will not necessarily work in the future.
- You will learn how diversity can matter even more than ability in problem-solving contexts.
- This course will share with you the theoretical and empirical evidence that underpin success and will offer practical lessons to improve how you think about the strategic makeup of any group.

Who Benefits from this Course?

This course is for any organisation who wants its people to improve their fact-based thinking skills. People of varying skill levels up to and including CEOs and board members from many different industry verticals attend the course. Both the individuals and the companies sending them on the course experience the benefits of the training. This course is recommended for:

- Research and Development Personnel
- Marketing and Business Development
- Sales and Customer Service Personnel
- Human Resources
- Experienced Managers taking on new responsibilities
- Senior Staff and Role Models
- Team Leaders & Supervisors
- Senior Management
- Executive Management
- Department Heads
- C-suite executives
- Board members
- Business owners

We customise- the course to every level and audience depending on your requirements.

How is this Course Delivered?

We fine-tune and customise this program for your organisation's training needs. You will save your organisation's time, resources and money by us coming to you and delivering the training at your premises or a location determined to be ideal for your needs and desired outcomes. The Hidden Factor training course, is nearly always best delivered in two days. It can be truncated to a one-day program if required, but this requires, obviously, some content, case studies, and problem-challenges to be removed.

How many Delegates can Attend?

Typically, we suggest a maximum of 40 people from your organisation attend the training at any one time. This is a highly engaging and interactive training program. Larger groups can be accommodated, however, and we can structure the training to best meet your requirements.

Business Development, Marketing & Sales Training

Marketing Wisdom

How to Attract, Influence and Retain Clients Even If You Hate Selling

All programs are designed, written and produced to your organisation's specific requirements.

What You Will Learn

Based on the best-selling book written by Ric Willmot and published by Wiley, the Marketing Wisdom training course guides those responsible for marketing on how to build a quality client base of which your competitors would be proud. With this workshop, delegates learn every aspect and skill required to build and grow a successful business by attracting quality clients who pay handsome fees. You will discover how to identify or create your special market niche, how to initially contact a prospective client, gather the necessary data, reach conceptual agreement with the client (even before a proposal is offered), write a proposal that's geared towards receiving a positive response, and even how to dominate and own the sector specific to your area of expertise in the marketplace.

In this course, we examine how you can assimilate the knowledge needed to help your clients with their issues, problems, and decisions, and always be dead honest with them. This program guarantees that you will succeed in your marketing, business development, and selling endeavours because you will become of such tremendous value to your customers that they assimilate with you and come to depend on you and your organisation. This course delivers a unique and comprehensive marketing blueprint specifically designed to take full advantage of *Willmot's Whirlpool Marketing System*.

Every one of our training programs is uniquely designed and tailored to meet your specific circumstances and objectives.

Topic Menu includes but is not limited to:

- Identify the customers you want and deserve.
- Assess the long-term value of a client.
- Determine the value of a customer beyond direct income.
- Generalise or specialise?
- Strategies for isolating new targets of opportunity.
- Why you're the best choice for your market niche.
- Increase sales or fees using 29 proven techniques.
- Thought Leadership to attract buyers.
- You are in the Relationship Business.
- Establish great acquisition sources and dominate your market.
- Why you must provide value early.
- Attract clients to you.
- Reach out laterally to maximise effort.
- Develop market share without spending a fortune.
- How to win repeat business, referrals, and recommendations.
- Control selling conversations by asking questions.
- Build additional support for your work.
- Rules for results in relationships and proposals.
- Selective acquisition: choose the keepers and release the others.
- How and when to raise your prices.
- The hidden dangers of discounting.

How You Will Stand to Benefit as an Organisation

The primary aim of this course is to guide those responsible for sales, business development, customer relationships, marketing, advertising, public relations, etc., to ethically and exponentially grow customer numbers and sales revenues — and keep them. Business benefits as reported by previous course attendees include:

- Understand the effective marketing tactics and strategies for professionals.
- We examine easy-to-implement marketing tactics and strategies for any size firms in any industry.
- Negates the need for expensive and often ineffective external marketing or sales consultants or branding and public relations firms.
- Make use of both traditional and up-to-the-minute digital marketing tools.
- Write winning proposals tailored to each client's needs and goals.

Who Benefits from this Course?

This course is for anyone in organisational life who interacts with or is responsible for clients and customers and building business opportunities and revenues. We've had hundreds of people of varying skill levels from new managers to CEOs from many different industry verticals attend the course. Both the individuals and the companies sending them on the course experience the benefits of the training. This course is recommended for:

- Customer service and care staff
- Relationship Managers
- Sales and Business Development
- Account, territory and country sales and business development representatives
- Advertising, public relations, marketing
- Middle Management
- Executive Management
- Senior Managers & Department Heads
- C-suite executives
- Board members
- Business owners

We customise- the course to every level and audience depending on your requirements.

How is this Course Delivered?

We fine-tune and customise this program for your organisation's training needs. You will save your organisation's time, resources and money by us coming to you and delivering the training at your premises or a location determined to be ideal for your needs and desired outcomes. The Marketing Wisdom training course, based on your requirements, ranges from two to four days.

How many Delegates can Attend?

Typically, we suggest a maximum of 30 people from your organisation attend the training at any one time. This is a highly engaging and interactive training program. Larger groups can be accommodated, however, and we can structure the training to best meet your requirements.

I have been engaging Ric's professional services since 2013. Known as "The Strategist", Ric is very skilful, knowledgeable, sensible, thoughtful and a pleasure to work with. Always giving more than expected, willing to spend his valuable time when you need him the most and very generous in sharing his knowledge. If you are in need to improve your business strategies, he is the man that you should be looking for!
— **Sara Andies, Executive Development Programmes at TinkSpace, Malaysia**

Business Development, Marketing & Sales Training
Guerrilla Marketing Bootcamp
Turbocharge Your Marketing Performance

What You Will Learn

At the completion of this 2-Day Learning Program, you will have developed an Action Plan for your marketing that you can immediately implement. You will also have an intimate knowledge of what works and what doesn't: all the powerful, proven tactics distilled down into a 29-Step plan. It will be your dynamic blueprint to maximise profits and increase customer numbers. You will know how to take your business to the next level with speed and efficiency.

This is a structured Bootcamp and is designed for organisations of all types. In this course you have the potential to transform how you market, compete, provide service, advertise, and sell. You will discover that your potential is already within you and that marketing success has less to do with budget and almost everything to do with intelligence, savvy, and action.

During the course you will be required to develop action steps, participate in role plays, engage in strategy discussions, and ultimately immerse yourself in the learning and share with the group. You will be video-taped and your recorded performances will be dissected and critiqued by the course facilitator and your fellow delegates. You will then be required to retake the video session and improve on your previous performance. All delegates will be sent a copy of Ric Willmot's book: Marketing Wisdom and will be required to read the book before the commencement of the two-day training program.

This program, unlike nearly all of our other programs, does not need to be tuned or modified.

Topics:

- Develop a masterful marketing mindset.
- Make a commitment or stand aside.
- Developing Purpose with Objectives, Focus and Prioritisation.
- Uncovering the opportunities through intelligent research.
- Target marketing: Narrowing your field.
- Positioning: Maximise and capitalise on your strengths.
- Features versus benefits.
- Create a fundamental value proposition.
- The importance of communication.
- Key Performance Indicators versus Key Result Areas.
- Willmot's Marketing Whirlpool.
- Time management.
- Customer Assessment & Profiling.
- Turning cold calls into warm welcomes.
- Purposeful pricing strategies.
- Community Involvement & Association Membership.
- Testimonials; Referrals; Customer Service ; and Word-of-mouth.
- Networking Smart for Results.

- Frequent buyer programs.
- Premium and special gifts.
- Trade shows.
- Do you need a blog?
- Social Media.

How You Will Stand to Benefit as an Organisation

The approach of this course is straightforward: You learn the content and develop the structure and process on how that content directly relates to your role and your organisation. By the conclusion of the two days you will have developed an action plan specifically tailored for you, your role, your organisation. Business benefits as reported by previous course attendees include:

- Developing a marketing mindset that encompasses all facets of your products and services, and your customers and markets.
- You will learn how to assess the worth and long-term value of your customers. This enables you to determine where to look for more quality customers and which customers you will necessarily let go and have them leave your business.
- Understanding that marketing directly links in with time management. Planning your marketing activity so it is a natural activity in your working day, every day with being burdensome.
- This course will teach you how the "sales rules" of the past will not necessarily work in the future. And, what you must do about it to remain relevant in the new age of ethical selling.
- This Bootcamp will help you to cease wasting ridiculous sums of money on failed advertising and promotions that don't produce a serious Return on Investment.

Who Benefits from this Course?

This course is for any organisation who wants its people to improve their fact-based thinking skills. People of varying skill levels up to and including CEOs and board members from many different industry verticals attend the course. Both the individuals and the companies sending them on the course experience the benefits of the training. This course is recommended for:

- Marketing and Business Development
- Sales and Customer Service Personnel
- Call centre personnel
- Anyone who has direct customer contact
- Experienced Managers taking on new responsibilities
- Senior Staff and Role Models
- Team Leaders & Supervisors
- Senior Management
- Executive Management
- C-suite executives
- Business owners

How is this Course Delivered?

You will save your organisation's time, resources and money by us coming to you and delivering the training at your premises or a location determined to be ideal for your needs and desired outcomes. The Guerrilla Marketing Bootcamp, is delivered in two consecutive days.

How many Delegates can Attend?

Typically, we suggest a maximum of 20 people from your organisation attend the training at any one time. This is because the program entails a large amount of group work, role plays, case studies, and video recording and review. This is a highly engaging and interactive training program. If larger numbers need to be accommodated, we recommend delivering the programs of 20 participants each, back-to-back.

Cursing the darkness?

Are you and your business lighting candles or cursing the darkness, **Ric Willmot** asks

Peter Finch's character's famous admonition in the movie *Network* embodies the degree of indignation that has at long last overcome consumer torpor in the past.

There are some mechanisms that allow the fury to be vented. The Telecommunications Ombudsman, for instance, receives hundreds of thousands of complaints about mobile phone carriers and marketers.

But it is a rare watchdog, necessitated by clear issues of fraud and misconduct within a burgeoning growth market.

Many critics state that even this government body has blunted teeth, vacillating and deferring any action on behalf of a powerless victim.

There are only three categories of impetus for an organisation to consistently do the right thing by its customers:
1. A set of corporate values and a philosophy that mandates quality and unqualified responsiveness to customer need.
2. Customer feedback so horrendously aggravating that it is easier to comply than it is to keep battling with them.
3. Petitions to those whose self-interest is threatened by consumer fury, and who possess power to terrify offenders.

The InterContinental Hotel chain is, perhaps, the ambassador for category 1, offering exceptional facilities, training and incentivising its people in unqualified customer service.

Just this month, while in Jakarta, the hotel's limousine service failed to collect me from the airport. I was offered no excuses, the blame was not laid elsewhere, and I was not referred on to a front desk manager. What was offered was full payment in restitution for my costs of arranging my own limousine, an honest apology, along with a bottle of wine and a tray of chocolates in my suite the next evening.

Category 2 is represented by consumer advocacy groups that have been responsible for voluntary recalls of toys or household electrical goods and appliances.

Category 3 is usually reserved for either politically sensitive issues or such widespread unhappiness that virtually all customers can be affected.

Why is it that some organisations strive to deliver the epitome of quality and service while another believes good enough is enough? The reason is you and me!

The tolerance of mediocrity is a corrupting philosophy. As we permit expectations to deteriorate we encourage standards to conjointly degenerate as well.

Anyone who answers a phone in an organisation should 'own' what follows. "That's not my department" is an oxymoron, because resolving those issues is everyone's job.

Reluctance to empower people creates a closed loop system in which management is overwhelmed with working not to empower people and consumed with reluctant tasks. No one gets developed in this system, so satisfaction, job expansion, careers and aspirations can't be advanced.

This results in at best diffident and, at worst, apathetic staff who perform poorly.

Such employees are the last people in the world whom management would want to empower, so the circle is complete.

If your business is to be a leader in establishing quality and aggressively raising those same standards, what are the hallmarks of excellence to be extolled?

Does your organisation base its reputation and responsiveness upon what is right ethically or what is expedient financially?

Does it provide recognition to people who fail trying to do the right thing?

Can employees articulate the values that influence their behaviour every day?

Do you 'shop' your own organisation and determine if it easy to business with?

Do requests and complaints to the organisation get addressed and solved by the first person contacted?

Many people complain about how disgraceful customer service conditions have become. Relatively few are constantly improving whatever they can within their organisation. Are you lighting candles or cursing the darkness?

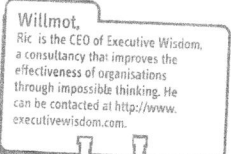

Willmot,
Ric is the CEO of Executive Wisdom, a consultancy that improves the effectiveness of organisations through impossible thinking. He can be contacted at http://www.executivewisdom.com.

Sailing to Success

By Ric Willmot

When the Spanish explorer, Hernando Cortes landed at Veracruz, he immediately burned his ships. He said to his sailors: "You can fight or you can die". Burning his ships removed the third option: ceding and sailing back to Spain. Now and then it requires greater creativity to eradicate excuses than it does to come up with the idea. In business, there never seems to be a shortage of ideas. Being visionary isn't as difficult as you may think. But transforming the vision you have today into reality tomorrow requires intelligent and pragmatic action. Success is predetermined by the implementation and nothing happens until you do something.

In 1986 Eric G. Flamholtz wrote the book, How to Make the transition from an Entrepreneurship to a Professionally Managed Firm, in which he discussed managing the stages of organisational growth.

One of the critical challenges facing a rapidly growing entrepreneurial company is to cope simultaneously with the endless day-to-day problems of a developing organisation while keeping an eye on its future direction ... and this is, in many ways, akin to navigating unchartered waters in a leaky rowboat with an inexperienced crew while surrounded by a school of sharks. The sea is unfamiliar, the boat is clumsy, the skills needed are not readily apparent or not fully developed, and there is a constant reminder of the high costs of an error in judgement.

There are prerequisites that any and all organisations must accomplish to be successful. Interestingly, many organisations are doing some of what's required without specifically attributing them as Key Result Areas (KRAs) necessary for operational excellence. Troubled organisations, or organisations that are not fulfilling the level of performance expected will usually be those entities who have failed to identify these prerequisites, attribute appropriate emphasis on them, and/or have failed to implement at varying stages in the organisation's development.

These prerequisites are far from being merely theoretical. Indeed, the understanding of why they're important and valid is based on the analysis of both successful and unsuccessful organisations, their effectiveness, and the experiences of the executives in charge. They are in order:

1. Identification and definition of a viable market niche;
2. Development of products and/or services appropriate to the organisation's chosen market niche;
3. and/or development of the resources required to operate the firm;
4. Development of the operational systems necessary for the firm to function on a day-to-day basis;
5. Development of the management systems required for the overall functioning of the organisation on a long-term basis; and
6. Development of the organisational culture that management feels is necessary to guide the business.

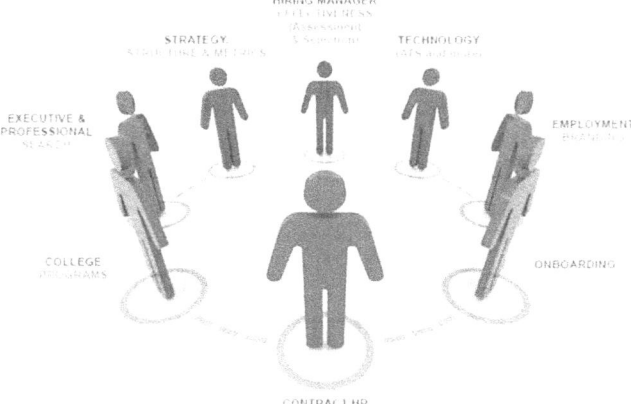

There is considerable myth propagated by self-proclaimed business gurus and experts extolling their own singular views of what makes an enterprise truly successful. Ask 10 of these experts for their personal definition of what is a successful business strategy and you will receive 17 answers. In my consulting experience I've been witness to many strategy reviews by organisations that sometimes amount to little more than business tourism. The executive committee jets in for the day, sees the sites, meets the natives, and jets out. Transforming today's vision into tomorrow's reality requires substantively more effort than a day of PowerPoint presentations.

Microsoft, the world's leading software maker, is a matrix organisation where no strategy can be effectively executed without careful coordination across multiple functions and across two or more of Microsoft's seven business units. In 2004, CEO Steve Ballmer asked Robert Uhlaner, Microsoft's corporate vice president of strategy, planning, and analysis, to devise a new strategic planning process for the company. Uhlaner put in place a Growth in Performance Planning Process that starts with agreement by Ballmer's leadership team on a set of strategic themes. Turning your vision into reality requires continuous strategic development, similar to Microsoft's that effectively allows senior executives to focus on one issue at a time until they reach a decision on how to go-to-market. This is in essence continuous, decision-oriented planning.

It is often suggested that an organisation requires a Unique Selling Proposition (USP). But not every enterprise can become another Apple. Not every CEO can be a clone of Steve Jobs. As an example of how you can be successful without being unique, Dreyer, a manufacturer of ice cream (which is certainly not unique) grew sales from $14.4 million in 1978 to $55.8 million in 1982 by cultivating a market niche between the premium Haagen-Dazs and generic supermarket brands. The ability to identify and define a specific market niche with exceptional clarity is the foundation prerequisite for organisational success.

While many organisations have the ability to correctly assess current and future market needs, not all organisations are able to develop a product and/or service offering that is capable of adequately satisfying that need. It's not enough to decide upon your market niche. Organisations have to be able to succeed in the process of productisation where not only does the enterprise design the product or service for the market niche, but it has the ability to produce it. If the offering is a service then the organisation must implement a "service delivery system", which is mechanism through which the firm provides the "tangible-purchase" to clients.

The third prerequisite is the acquisition and/or development of the resources required and this is a major task that organisations face in creating real results from the strategic vision. The capability of an organisation to fulfil its vision hinges on its ability to acquire the competent capacity to fulfil production requirements. Not only must the organisation have the capability, but it must be perceived by the marketplace to be confident and capable to deliver. The organisation has to be an exemplar of what it produces.

It will be difficult, if not impossible, for prospective clients to purchase financial planning advice from an organisation suffering its own financial difficulties. Nobody is going to trust a dentist with bad teeth, or a swim coach who won't get in the water.

Paradoxically, success can create unwanted problems with regards to resources. For example, a small organisation competing in the manufacture of fast moving consumer goods (FMCG) necessarily needs to maintain a low cost of production. But as demand and sales increase, so does

> "While turning today's vision into tomorrow's reality requires pragmatic, intelligent prerequisites, it also needs you to be brave and take risks."

the requirement for automation in the manufacturing process, which small firms cannot afford to purchase. The organisation's success in identifying a market niche will create increased demand for its product and services. Thereby stretching the organisation's resources. This, in turn, places additional burden upon the organisation to increase its physical resources such as equipment, storage, production facilities, human resources, etc. It's ironic that the organisation's own success is the catalyst for its own new set of problems.

At this point, the effectiveness of operational systems to be able to efficiently deliver is a confronting challenge. This is an area that can be easily neglected by management and incredibly difficult to repair before it destroys organisational performance and decimates the repute of the business both internally and externally. Many organisations experience business growth at a pace that outstrips existing administrative systems. During periods of growth there is an ever-increasing workload assigned to financial, administrative, marketing, human resources, and service delivery systems. If these systems are not capable of easily coping with business growth then the organisation exposes itself to serious business disruption and possibly a cultural catastrophe.

GLOBAL LEARNING FOR A GLOBAL AUDIENCE

Those responsible for business development and sales will become frustrated and incensed when the delivery of products and services is not made within promised timeframes because the organisation's manufacturing, inventory, logistics, and the like are grossly inadequate or incorrect.

These are all symptoms of disconnect between the vision of what is possible and the reality of what is doable.

- People within organisations that I consult with may tell me things like, "There is just not enough time in a day."
- I will observe middle managers continually problem-solving and putting out fires.
- My analysis of the financials will show that as the business has continued to grow sales, profits have not.
- Employees begin to have many more frequent sick days and there is a genuine sense of insecurity about the future.

These are all key indicators of an organisation suffering from growing pains.

Medieval map makers would draw a dragon at the edges of the 'known world' to indicate that any travellers would be entering unknown territories and did so at their own risk. The famous copper Lenox Globe (c. 1503-07) bears the phrase 'HC SVNT DRACONES' (Latin for 'Here are dragons') around the east coast of Asia. Many sailors and explorers took the advice literally and were either warned off venturing into these regions or did so believing they risked provoking the ire of the dragons and sea-monsters that lived there. For some brave people the dragon indicated opportunity and a gateway to wonderful lands to be discovered and explored.

While turning today's vision into tomorrow's reality requires pragmatic, intelligent prerequisites, it also needs you to be brave and take risks. You can't afford to be a victim of the tides and winds, so eschew the excuses, the cliches, and self-proclaimed gurus and set sail for your chosen port of call.

Ric Willmot is the Managing Director of Executive Wisdom Consulting Group. He is an expert in organisational productivity and performance with extensive experience in accounting, financial planning and organisational development consulting.
Email: info@executivewisdom.com
Website: http://executivewisdom.com
Blog: http://ricwillmot.com

Short-Course Programs
Design Your Own Programs
Generating Rapid Results with Short Courses

Your organisation can tailor in-house training by selecting from this menu of topics. Each topic ranges from 90 minutes to two hours in length. You would, therefore, choose three or four topics for a one-day program, six to eight topics for a two-day program, and so forth. These short courses are designed and delivered to be highly interactive, where your people become involved in in-depth discussions by answering questions posed to them by the facilitator to generate solutions-thinking specific to your organisation.

21st Century Talent Spotting

— *Identifying, Acquiring, Promoting, and Retaining the Leaders Your Organisation Needs for the Future*

- How organisational talent spotting has evolved over time.
- How to push people to excel.
- What matters today?
- What is Potential?
- How to retain good people.

Asserting Yourself at Work

— *Gain increased confidence and control*

- Improve your ability to handle potentially difficult situations.
- Knowing to identify when assertive behaviour is perceived as aggressive.
- Communicating in difficult situations; including how to keep calm when under pressure in a confrontational situation.
- Confidently dealing with implied or overt criticism.
- Techniques to achieve assertive behaviour.
- Express yourself more clearly.
- Tips to achieve improved confidence.

Be a Better Leader

— *Be better to yourself*

- Life is not a zero-sum game.
- Total Leadership Process.
- Identify possibilities.
- Adapt as you go.
- Finding support.
- Small steps for big change.

Blue Ocean Strategy
— *Understanding and using it for your organisation*

- An example of defying the odds.
- Red versus Blue.
- Blue Oceans are nothing new.
- Why do some companies still focus on Red Oceans?
- A shift in mindset.

Build an Innovation Engine in 90 Days
— *How to establish a system for creating innovation using a lean process*

- The minimum viable innovation system.
- Define your innovation buckets.
- Zero in on a few opportunities.
- Form a small development team.
- Metrics.
- Create a way to shepherd projects.

Can You Say What Your Strategy Is?
— *It's impossible to execute a strategy if you don't know what it is*

- Gaining clarity.
- The Strategy Statement.
- Strategic Intent.
- Objective.
- Scope.
- Competitive Advantage.
- The Sweet Spot.
- Get the words right.

Get Your Team to Do What It Says It's Going to Do
— *If-Then Planning*

- There's only a 50% success rate of intention to action.
- What stands in our way?
- Closing the gap.
- Steps to creating an If-Then Plan.
- Goals and objectives.

Hidden Traps in Decision Making
— *The traps that affect our results and outcomes*

- The Anchoring Trap.
- We prefer things to stay the same.
- Sunk Cost Bias.
- Confirmation Bias.
- Overconfidence.
- The way we state the problem influences our decision.
- Padding estimates doesn't pay off.
- Previous experiences impact future decisions.

How Management Teams Can Have a Good Fight

— *Managing conflict in teams*

- Focus on facts.
- Multiply the alternatives.
- Create common goals.
- Find a sense of humour.
- Balance the power structure.
- Seek qualified consensus.

How Netflix Reinvented HR

— *Changing what HR does to be more relevant*

- Stellar talent and stellar success.
- Hire only grown-ups.
- Cheerleading doesn't improve the morale.
- Tell the truth about performance.
- What skills will your team need in six months?
- Create your culture, your way.

International Negotiations

— *Cross-cultural negotiations*

- Tailor the way you express disagreement.
- Know when to hold and when to call.
- How does their culture build trust?
- Avoid the binaries.
- Understand the role of contracts.
- Have someone who understands the other culture.

Know Your Customers' "Jobs to Be Done"

— *How to identify new opportunities*

- Jobs aren't only tasks—they involve experiences.
- Circumstances versus characteristics.
- Look for more solutions.
- Social and emotional dimensions.
- Aligning processes.
- How can you uncover jobs to be done?

Leading the Team You Inherit

— *The challenge of leading an established team*

- 3 Steps to Team Transformation.
- Explain what you're looking for.
- Zero in on critical roles.
- Urge high-performance behaviour.
- Alignment with a clear purpose.
- Rethink how people work.
- Accelerate team development.

Make Time for Work That Matters
— *Increasing personal productivity and efficiency*

- Think more deliberately.
- Find the 25%.
- Identify low-value tasks.
- Drop, delegate, or redesign.
- What should you be doing instead?
- Commit.

Making Exit Interviews Count
— *How to achieve strategic benefits*

- Why are Exit Interviews ineffective?
- Start at the end and work back.
- Create lifelong advocates for your organisation.
- Defining Who, When, and How.
- Rules of engagement.
- After the Interview.

Managers Becoming Leaders
— *Stepping into your first leadership role*

- Get out of your comfort zone.
- Moving from Analyst to Integrator.
- Let go of the tactical issues.
- Think in terms of systems.
- Problem solver to agenda setter.
- Becoming a diplomat.

Marketing Myopia
— *Your product is NOT your business*

- There's no such thing as a growth industry.
- Focus on customers' needs, not your capabilities.
- Growth is NOT guaranteed.
- There will always be a substitute.
- Mass production won't protect you.
- An overemphasis on R&D.

Navigating the Cultural Minefield
— *You're now a small part of a global village*

- Communication-Context.
- Evaluating one another.
- Points of persuasion.
- Decisions, decisions, no decisions.
- It's a matter of trust.
- Scheduling time: "Just a suggestion."
- Old habits die hard.
- One size does not fit all.

Reinventing Performance Management
— Focus on the future not the past

- The Review Process is a Time Sink.
- Ratings are mostly a reflection of the reviewer.
- Finding a better system.
- Reward good performance.
- See performance clearly.
- Future Focus.
- A shift in approach.

Reinventing Your Business Model
— Elements of success

- Why is reinventing your business model so difficult?
- Elements of a successful business model.
- Customer Value Proposition.
- Profit Formula.
- Do you need a new model?
- Opportunities and Needs.
- Be patient for growth — but impatient for profit.

Saving Rookie Managers From Themselves
— Identifying and correcting problems

- What got you here, isn't going to get you there.
- Delegation.
- Support from above.
- Projecting Confidence.
- The big picture.
- Giving Feedback.

Set-Up-To-Fail Syndrome
— How managers unwittingly undermine their direct reports

- Micromanagement signals low expectations.
- The In-Crowd versus the Out-Crowd.
- Tight controls dampen motivation.
- Gaining the right context.
- Symptoms versus Cause
- Gap analysis.
- The new path forward.
- Honest communication.
- Prevention is the best option.

Six Habits of Merely Effective Negotiators
— Ways to increase your effectiveness as a negotiator

- Neglecting the other party.
- Emotion versus Economics.
- Positions versus Interests.
- Differences can open the door.
- BATNA.
- Skewed vision: Biases .

.

The Authenticity Paradox
— *Trust, Truth, and Engagement*

- WANTED: Believable leaders.
- Your identity should guide you forward but not fence you in.
- Surviving the first 90 days.
- Transparent executive's quandary.
- Selling yourself: a hard reality.
- Create a new story.
- Your personal narrative.

The Discipline of Business Experimentation
— *Innovations don't always pay off*

- Does the experiment have a clear purpose?
- Do your stakeholders have buy-in?
- Is the experiment doable?
- Can you ensure reliable results?
- Have you gotten the most value out of the experiment?
- It all comes down to rigor.

The Focused Leader
— *How leaders must focus their attention*

- The assault on attention.
- Self-awareness.
- Developing self-control.
- Empathy and relationships.
- Explorative strategic thinking.
- Putting it all together.

The Lean Start-up
— *Why it changes everything*

- The business model canvas.
- Customer development.
- Agile product development.
- Ramp up operations quickly.
- Barriers to start-up formation.
- The Past versus

The New Science of Customer Emotions
— *Using emotional motivators to grow a business*

- Customer satisfaction is not enough.
- Emotionally connected customers.
- Emotional motivators.
- How to build emotional connections.
- Analyse your connected customers.
- Don't rely on demographics alone.
- Optimise all functions and touchpoints.
- Systematise, Measure, and Learn.

The Real Leadership Lessons of Steve Jobs

— *It's not about his personality but his accomplishments*

- What NOT to do.
- Simplify.
- Take responsibility.
- When behind, leapfrog.
- Put products before profits.
- Don't be a slave to focus groups.
- Bend reality.
- Customers judge a book by its cover.
- Insist on perfection.
- Tolerate only "A" players.
- Engage face-to-face.
- Big picture and details.
- Combine humanities with science.
- Stay hungry, stay foolish.

The Science of Persuasion

— *Tactics for leaders to motivate performance*

- People like those who like them.
- People repay in kind.
- People defer to experts.
- People follow the lead of those who are similar to them.
- People stick to commitments made publicly.
- People want more of what is less available.
- Dishonesty doesn't work.

Time is Money

— *And, it's your scarcest organisational resource*

- The stakes are high.
- Set clear priorities.
- Use zero-based time budgeting.
- Simplify the organisation.
- Initiative-Creep: Demand business cases for projects.
- Standardise Decision Rights.
- Meeting Discipline.

What Great Managers Do

— *A review of the behaviours of top performers*

- Capitalise on uniqueness.
- Build upon strengths.
- People care most about recognition.
- How do people prefer to learn?
- Tell the truth, even when it hurts.
- You must have bench-strength.
- It's why we have scoreboards in sport.

What Makes a Leader?

— *Emotional intelligence is vital for every leader*

- Judging capabilities.
- Controlling disruptive impulses with self-regulation.
- Making the drive to excel contagious.
- Environment of fairness and trust.
- You don't need to be loved.
- Relationship building.
- Friendliness with a purpose.

Why Organisations Don't Learn

— *Organisational learning is crucial but difficult to sustain*

- Do leaders mean what they say?
- Embrace a growth mindset.
- Overreliance on past performance.
- Bias toward action.
- Tired workers aren't good learners.
- Push past obvious fixes.
- Norms can stifle innovation.
- Empower workers to use knowledge.

Why Strategy Execution Unravels

— *And what to do about it*

- Does Execution equal Alignment?
- Executive Bias.
- Limited thinking when under pressure.
- Being agile doesn't mean chasing every opportunity.
- People don't get the strategy.
- Redefine execution.

Executive Wisdom has delivered training and consulting services to professional associations, government departments, NGOs, and corporations around the world. We regularly work in:

- Australia
- Brunei
- Canada
- Fiji
- Hong Kong
- Indonesia
- Japan
- Malaysia
- New Zealand
- Papua New Guinea
- Philippines
- Singapore
- South Africa
- South Korea
- Thailand
- United Arab Emirates
- United States of America

CONSULTING

Since 2004, Executive Wisdom Consulting Group has been assisting organisations to improve performance and productivity by working collaboratively, incorporating the staff members and organisational resources together with the transference of learnable skills to the client. We serve our clients at every level of their organisation—from trusted advisor to top management, to hands-on coach for front line supervisors and team leaders. We are ambitious for our clients—we work with them to achieve their full potential and become even better than they already are.

Executive Wisdom Consulting Group works towards specific objectives with clearly established outcomes and timing, purposely contributing to the clients' goals. Our approach revolves around a simple concept: improving the client's condition. Past experience and results indicate that improved performance necessarily requires investment in people, systems and support mechanisms. However, that investment may not need additional resources, but rather the redeployment of talents, resources, and energy already present.

Our experience and training guide us as to how and by what means we can contribute most. We draw upon the knowledge including Open Systems Thinking, Action Research, Process Design, Jungian philosophy, NLP, and Adaptive Systems. This allows Executive Wisdom Consulting Group to bring a wide range of solutions and responses to bear on the needs of the client organisation. Underlying is a belief that people congregate together in organisations and communities to fulfil some overarching goal and to meet their own needs. We view our client organisations as multi-layered living systems with a life of their own, independent of the individuals that constitute them.

"Being clear about what you want from organisational change is one thing, designing effective methods and processes to accomplish it while being focused on results is another."

What Executive Wisdom Does For Your Organisation

Customer Strategy & Marketing

Customer insights and segmentation: We help clients understand customer needs and behaviours using our Willmot's Marketing Whirlpool® approach and develop actionable segmentation from the resulting insights. We help clients define the target customer or "sweet spot"—the area of distinct advantage over competitors—to inform business decisions and investment allocation.

Product and category management: We help firms break down barriers to innovation and improve ongoing customer-led product development, so their value proposition is differentiated and meets customer needs.

Pricing: We help resolve the pricing paradox—pricing is almost always the #1 profit lever, yet it remains under-developed in most companies—by building long-term pricing capabilities and capitalising on in-year-revenue opportunities.

Sales and channel effectiveness: We help companies identify quick, targeted, customised solutions as well as strategic and operational improvements to boost underperforming sales organisations.

Marketing strategy: We help companies align their marketing strategy with overarching business objectives; ensure marketing investments are generating highest returns and reinforcing the brand positioning; and build a loyal customer base through branding that cultivates a reliable, trusted image.

Customer experience: We work with companies to develop a series of positive interactions with the customer to earn their advocacy and inform the consistent delivery of experiences to drive top-line growth.

Loyalty: We help companies nurture advocates—loyal customers who are more profitable, and who are active proponents of your business in good times and bad.

Go-to-market strategy: We help companies create powerful, integrated go-to-market systems that build a bridge between a company's strategy and the exceptional customer experiences that are the ultimate driver of customer advocacy and loyalty.

We help companies at every stage of growth, developing custom solutions and collaborating with all levels of the organisation.

Merger & Acquisitions

Executive Wisdom helps companies improve their odds of successful Mergers & Acquisitions through an integrated, battle-tested approach that links acquisition strategy, diligence and merger integration.

Based on our analysis and experience—including firsthand experiences of Ric Willmot while he was the CEO of a company that acquired three other organisations over five years—our mergers and acquisitions experts believe that the key to successful M&A is a repeatable model; one that companies can return to over and over again to reap substantial rewards.

Mergers and Acquisitions begin by building a robust capability that becomes the foundation for the success of the model's five key steps:

Corporate strategy and acquisition strategy: Develop an articulated strategy and an M&A plan that reinforces that strategy. Strategy is Ric Willmot's heritage; with more than 13 years of experience helping companies develop strategies, he understands the types of deals that create value and those that don't.

Deal thesis: Invest with a thesis. Successful deals are guided by a meaningful deal thesis that is tied to a firm's growth strategy and that spells out how the deal will add value both to the target and acquiring company.

Strategic due diligence: Ask and answer the big questions. The best acquirers investigate targets for what's important, identifying the critical sources of ongoing value. A frequent acquirer knows precisely where it can add value and is, therefore, able to set its price—and to walk away if the price isn't right.

Merger integration planning: Integrate where it matters. No two integrations are the same, and companies must carefully consider aspects of culture to IT to realise the full value of the deal.

Merger integration execution: Nail the short list of critical actions. Merging two companies requires rigorous follow-through on a long list of integration tasks, large and small. Doing both is hard. Part of the answer lies in a few, powerful guiding principles: tailor the integration thesis to the deal thesis; integrate where it matters, and act with deliberate speed.

Executive Wisdom's mergers and acquisitions consultants help companies build and execute on their repeatable models for M&A. We also apply our expertise to guide companies and management teams that are deciding where to grow and shed through joint ventures and alliances or divestitures and separations.

Our work is continually informed by the latest M&A analyses and insights which ensure that our clients have access to information and conclusions about how the best acquirers succeed.

Organisational Development

Some organisations work. They accomplish what they set out to do, and their employees are engaged and happy with their jobs. However, Executive Wisdom research indicates that less than 20 percent of companies achieve that. Executive Wisdom helps clients improve financial performance and make their organisations better places to work by ensuring the entire organisation system is aligned and set up to deliver on the company's objectives.

Executive Wisdom has completed more than 100 organisational assignments in the last ten years. Our areas of expertise include:

Organisation Diagnostics: Executive Wisdom's diagnostic tools help clients assess and identify how to improve their organisational performance. We help companies determine where their organisation is strong, where it is weak and, most critically, which outcomes matter most for generating superior business performance.

Organisational design and operating model: A well-designed operating model provides a clear and consistent blueprint for how resources are organised and operated to achieve a company's strategic priorities. We partner with clients to help them design and implement operating models that translate strategy into effective execution.

Organisation Simplification: Organisational complexity is the new normal, driven by growth, globalisation and disruptive technologies; adequately addressing it requires time and focus. Our holistic approach helps companies identify and simultaneously address the fundamental drivers of complexity to ensure that its symptoms don't creep back.

Decision effectiveness: Executive Wisdom helps organisations determine problem. We help businesses strengthen weak elements of their organisation and embed ethical and proper decision making and execution into everyday operations.

Role of the C-suite: Examining the efforts of the C-suite helps CEOs and boards of companies with ineffectual structures determine the best organisational model for their firm. The C-suite must be "fit for purpose," with roles aligned to the company's business profile, strategy and leadership style. Executive Wisdom's focus is on value-added: Effectiveness is 90 percent of the game—making certain the right decisions get made by the right people at the right time. Efficiency is critical but secondary.

Talent management and leadership supply: No company can turn in a great performance without great people. High performers learn to assess their talent pipeline, deploy their most promising people more efficiently in critical decision areas and reduce their demand for scarce skills.

Measures and incentives: Executive Wisdom helps companies create dynamic performance measurement with a focus on what matters to the business. We review business performance and help companies devise tailored compensation systems that will reward actions and behaviours that advance the organisation's goals and drive decision effectiveness.

High-performance culture: Company culture is at the heart of competitive advantage because it determines how things are done and how people behave. It is the hardest thing for competitors to copy. High performers create an environment with a unique passion for performance—so that people make the right decisions wherever they reside in the business.

Change management: Change is tough and always has been. Organisational change is a particularly emotional process—often a source of tension and insecurity. "Will I still have a job?" "What will it be?" We help companies account for these sensitivities with clear communications and solid engagement plans to motivate people. Our approach draws from experiential learning about what actions make change stick. We help deliver "fast wins" by anchoring change in customer and marketplace needs and by tackling changes in parallel, and enduring success by building organisation alignment and avoiding ambiguity around critical roles and decision processes.

Leadership behaviours and alignment: Leadership behaviours are one of the critical "soft" elements that research shows are most important in determining an organisation's decision effectiveness and thus its performance. Sometimes, however, a company's leadership behaviours and decision style will have to change—adapting to a different strategy or perhaps the arrival of new leaders. The key to changing behaviours is reaching agreement on the desired style, and then defining and demonstrating the required practices.

Management process redesign: Well-executed processes are essential to a company's performance. Executive Wisdom's practical, structured approach to management processes helps drive faster, better decisions, more productive meetings, and efficient execution. We work with clients to develop tailored management practices and build the skills and behaviours that lead to enduring results.

Operations

How much better, faster or smarter could you do what you do? Executive Wisdom helps you reimagine your operations to unlock growth, lower costs and unleash your strategy. Our operations consulting experts have collaborated on over 130 projects providing a wealth of experience and real-world knowledge on achieving operational excellence.

What We Offer:

- We deliver tailored, actionable and pragmatic operational offerings.
- Lean Six Sigma: Reap the benefits of faster processes with lower waste and higher qualities.
- Service Design & Operations: Consistently deliver the customer promise at the right cost across service channels.

Our work is anchored on Ric Willmot's in-depth knowledge and proven approaches to change management.

Performance Improvement & Results Delivery

Traditional change management has been around for decades, but is the same old approach enough to make a difference? More than 70 percent of major change efforts fail. Executive Wisdom's approach helps clients overcome the odds by predicting, measuring and managing the risk associated with change management from day one. The result: unparalleled support from strategy to implementation that delivers sustained results.

What We Offer:

- **Coaching and Capability:** To improve your organisation's capacity for change and deliver the results of change programs.
- **Transformation Consulting:** Reenergise stalled or struggling transformations, helping you achieve full potential results.
- **Center for Business Excellence:** Unleash the collective power of your people to deliver innovative insights, cohesive teams and faster results.
- **Organisational Culture Change:** Prioritise the behaviours that matter most to your organisation's change program and inspire their adoption throughout the company, from the frontline to the executive suite.
- **Inspire & Rewire:** Coaching and developing senior leaders and teams to ensure that their shared purpose is reflected in the way they work with the broader organisation.
- **Change Management Consulting**: Executive Wisdom offers specialised tools to support leaders through change management programs and transformations.
- **Accelerated Financial Transformation:** Rapidly identify and capture revenue and cost savings opportunities when you urgently need a financial turnaround.
- **Complexity Management:** Reduce all forms of complexity to unlock value and turbocharge growth, agility and competitiveness.

Ric is a dynamic, engaging and energetic consultant who talks straight and gets things done. He's a natural communicator who makes sense to people at all levels of an organization.

Andrew Bass, Bass Clusker Consulting

Strategy

Are your competitors talking about you in their boardrooms? Does your strategy guide how you allocate resources? Can every employee articulate your strategic intent and are they empowered to execute on it? At Executive Wisdom, we see strategy as much more than a bulky planning document. We work with companies to develop strategies that deliver results. For more than 13 years, Executive Wisdom's superior capabilities have helped hundreds of clients create winning strategies.

We see things that others miss, offering you more creative solutions that combine our deep geographic experience, intimate sector knowledge and clear insights into how to create value in your business. We work collaboratively, build lasting capabilities into your team and help your organisation mobilise for change. We define our success by your results. We care deeply about our clients. We enjoy our work—and we have fun doing it.

Our strategy consulting expertise includes:

- **Fundamentals of Growth:** Only 1 in 9 companies succeed in achieving sustained growth. We help businesses grow by defining and focusing on their core.

- **Business Unit Strategy:** An effective strategy for business units requires making decisions about where to play and how to win. The goal is to enable a business to reach its full economic potential.

- **Corporate Strategy:** Corporate strategy involves a proprietary set of actions that enables a company to be worth more than just the sum of its parts.

- **Emerging markets:** Home to most of the world's population and recording double-digit growth, emerging markets in Asia and the Middle East are must-win areas for multinational companies. Executive Wisdom helps enterprises to navigate this unfamiliar terrain and successfully compete against indigenous companies and other multinationals.

Although extremely challenging and not afraid to speak his mind, Ric offered a level of business and marketing acumen you simply wouldn't be able to hire on a standard basis. He brought our marketing strategy into the 21st century and assisted in dramatically enhancing our bottom line.

GRAEME SMITH, Network 20

Elvis has left the building

While waiting for my order at the coffee shop, I atypically entered into a sports debate with one of the regulars.

He was extolling the latest exploits and the 300th game of the New Zealand Warriors League player, Ruben Wiki, one of the finest professional rugby league players ever to have played for that land across the ditch.

I created an unholy uproar with this supporter when I commented that Ruben was now embarrassing to watch, well past his prime.

My coffee shop cohort leapt from his chair.

"How can you say that?!" he roared. "Wiki past his prime is still better than 90 percent of the rest of the league!"

"Perhaps," I said, "but he has been selected for the Warrior's team as an act of mercy and memory while other more formidable players surrender their place to him."

"Listen," retorted my colleague, "he doesn't embarrass himself out there."

"Yes, but is that the goal in life — to go through it merely not embarrassing ourselves?"

That ended the discussion.

For every star and celebrity who goes out on top we have hundreds who hang on, faint outlines of their former profiles, echoes of their erstwhile resonance.

I've watched too many people at all levels embarrass and demean themselves in futile attempts to remain what they were a decade or more prior.

The critical factor isn't chronology but rather the competency and expertise to continue to perform at your best level, or to exceed that level.

Once that level is no longer rising, the laws of entropy enter, and the plateau will ineluctably erode.

> "BUSINESS LEADERS MUST BE COGNISANT THAT INNOVATION AND REINVENTION ARE TWO KEY IMPERATIVES FOR SUCCESS AND SURVIVAL"

Business leaders must be cognisant that innovation and reinvention are two key imperatives for success and survival.

The barrier to freely extolling this strategy for many senior executives and leaders is, as is currently happening, a stalled or declining economy.

The focus then is on cost cutting and efficiency.

This may help organisations weather the downturn, but this approach will ultimately render them obsolete.

What do we know for sure about reinvention and innovation?

Well, for starters, big mergers (by and large) don't work and therefore scale is over-rated.

Planning, most of the time, is activity over results; kind of like bureaucracy!

Expert predictions are rarely any more successful than roulette.

If you believe the memoirs of CEOs you should be institutionalised, because success stories are the illusions of egomaniacs.

How can we become more innovative and what are some of the ways we can gain inspiration for reinvention?

- Stop benchmarking; rather form alliances with entrepreneurial thinkers
- Use turnaround thinking – whatever you think, think the opposite and then consider the merits of that thinking
- Shred your newspaper clippings; you're never as good as your last victory, nor as bad as your last defeat
- Listen to your gut rather than statistics, planning and focus groups
- Have a "Be/Do" philosophy.
- Celebrate successful failures and punish mediocrity
- Diversify just for the heck of it
- Thrive on ambiguity, because if the answer is known, then it's no longer innovative, is it?
- Maintain accountability by cultivating your people to be "Dreamers with Deadlines"

Athletes become coaches; singers become actors; actors become directors; business people become entrepreneurs; entrepreneurs become teachers -- the potential for such "reinvention" of ourselves is boundless.

"Not embarrassing yourself" is never justification for continuing. The pursuit of higher levels of excellence is the justification for continuing.

Otherwise, we're still hanging out with Elvis and his impersonators in Las Vegas hoping to find shelter under our former shadow. But, meanwhile, the music has changed ...

RIC WILLMOT, known as "The Strategist" is dedicated to maximising the success, profitability and growth of businesses. You can subscribe to his free monthly e-zine, The Executive Wisdom Times at www.executivewisdom.com.

▶ FINANCIAL SUCCESS

Customer disservice

Customer service shouldn't be a poor man's cousin to growing your business. Have a strategy and stick to it, writes **Ric Willmot**

I called to speak with a previous seminar participant from Cairns who worked for a national tourist boat cruise company. The person who answered promptly informed me, "No, she quit two weeks ago!"

"May I speak to someone about booking a day-trip for my in-laws who will be in Cairns for a conference?"

"Transferring you."

New voice: "You want Alison's phone number?"

"Well no, I understand she has left the company. I want to book a day-cruise for my in-laws who will be in Cairns over Easter for a national conference."

"Call back on the number you originally dialed and speak with reservations." The phone was then disconnected before I could utter another word.

Disregard the obvious customer service implications: on two occasions, to separate people, I used the words "in Cairns for a conference".

1. What type of conference, Mr Willmot?
2. How many people are attending?
3. Are their spouses involved in any organised social outings whilst the conference is in action?

It just so happens that my father-in-law is an Executive Director for Toll North, one of Australia's largest logistics companies and there will be more than 600 delegates plus their spouses attending. Do you think the spouses might enjoy an arranged boat cruise out to the gorgeous Great Barrier Reef while their partners are slogging away in a conference hall?

You rarely awake in the morning with people waving cash in your face. So we have to market ourselves.

Unfortunately, many confuse the outcomes and results they wish to achieve with tasks and activities; means over ends.

We have all experienced poor customer service. Why? Attention needs to be paid to the internal workings of business that project externally.

What is the place you are trying to get your business to? The Allies didn't merely opt for a trip across the English Channel one day. Get your strategy clear, then ensure any task, program or procedure you implement reinforces that strategy. Support mechanisms must then effectively focus your attention. Here are my top five:

1. Prepare for success in acquiring new business.. Have the confidence to engage your clients and customers as a peer. My tailor can speak intelligibly to me about business and sport, or with another customer about the future of medical services.
2. Build relationships ... Nobody sells to monoliths. You do business with the people in those organisations. And behind every corporate objective is a personal objective. If you want to reach an emotional nexus with a client, find out why something is personally important.
3. Be ready for objections... "It's not in our budget/we don't have time right now/I have to ask." Familiar? Of course, so when you know these objections are coming, be prepared for them.
4. Gain marketshare ... Be bold in solutions and spare the diagnosis. I have never asked my doctor to explain how he came up with his diagnosis and the formula for the antidote — I just want to get better. Focus on improving the client's condition, not teaching them what you do. Provide options so the customer can choose ways of doing business with you. Find out the budget and always offer a higher option . If the high end denotes significant value to the customer, they may find the additional money. I call it the 'Porsche Paradox.'
5. Be prepared to walk away... Nothing can strengthen your position and guarantee a sale like your expressed willingness to walk away. Will you lose some customers? Yes. But you weren't getting the business anyway. If you did, it wasn't going to be profitable.

At one point during negotiations for the release of 15 British naval personnel, Iran's chief international negotiator Ali Larijani refused British officials' phone calls for days. If Iranians don't have an answer, they don't answer the phone. Clarify your strategy, define your approach, enhance your customer service, or don't answer the phone!■

Willmot, Ric, known as the "Consultant's Consultant", is the CEO of Executive Wisdom Consulting Group, a consultancy that improves the effectiveness of organisations through impossible thinking. www.executivewisdom.com

TYPICAL CLIENT RESULTS

Here are some recent examples from our hundreds of clients. This summarises a few of the identifiable projects designed and delivered, not the total gamut of our consulting for any of them.

Organisational Development

For **Gaby Cool Transport** we evaluated business operations to verify the best strategic focus necessary for continued success. This then served as the basis for the development of a growth strategy, peak performance management action plan, and an organisational process redesign.

Course Development

For **Bendigo Bank** we designed instructive workshops on leadership through to presentation skills, using specialised and purposely-created learning materials, and facilitated program sessions.

"Ric, thank you for your excellent presentation to our NSW and QLD Regional Managers on leadership. Your thought provoking and participative approach allowed our team (including myself) to reflect on our own leadership strengths, and how we can continue to learn and develop — and just as importantly, develop the skills of our teams. Thank you very much for preparing a high impact, clear, motivational and effective presentation."

Andrew Watts — Executive of Customer Service Improvement, Bendigo & Adelaide Bank

---

Innovation

For **Science 2 Medical** we designed a program to cultivate innovation throughout the entire organisation. This way the business units would operate innovatively as their market niche geographically became more globally diverse.

Human Resource Strategies

For **Sternhall Financial & Insurance** we appraised the staff competencies and accountabilities in relation to corporate objectives and contributed to their overall Human Resources strategy focusing on quantifiable and specific goals. Educational staff programs based upon business issues were developed, establishing an essential and comprehensible connection between staff training and organisational outcomes.

Problem Solving and Decision Making

For **Matilda Fuel Supplies** we designed and implemented a Professional Development Program for management personnel in the area of problem-solving and decision-making as it applies to human performance and strategy. This enabled management to determine the relationship between cause and effect and to subscribe their attention to cause-solution rather than symptom-attendance. One of the results being that management could address observed behaviour rather than inferred issues that have little or no consequence to business performance.

Strategy Design

For **LMW Insurance Brokers** we facilitated strategic sessions for the Directors and Senior Management, ensuring the organisation was able to allocate resources and prioritise plans. This allowed the company to preserve it's entrepreneurial quality, even as it implemented fundamental and indispensable systems crucial to safeguarding quality amidst extraordinary growth.

"Ric travelled to New Zealand and spoke to our team on two separate occasions. The response we received from all team members was fantastic. We all believe that as a direct result of his visits, our team is more focused, better at planning and keen to succeed. Without a doubt, Ric is one of the most impressive speakers we've ever heard. As a result, we have engaged him in strategic planning with our shareholder directors. This exercise and process undertaken have already resulted in some very measurable success. Ric's challenging analysis has resulted in some very profound changes in our organisation. He has helped focus us and provide us with the plan and the tools to grow. We intend to use Ric on an annual basis, both with our team and the directors. As well as being incredibly effective, he is also entertaining and a bloody nice guy."

Ken Williamson — Partner of Law Mooney Williamson Insurance Brokers, New Zealand

Re-engineering

For **Pacific Star Communications** we worked with senior staff to design and create pertinent management systems to fulfil expected consumer needs. To implement those management systems, we followed up with the introduction of team-building, management performance improvements, client evaluations, and customer feedback surveys. The project incorporated assessments of key managers and assistance in an advisory capacity on the acquisition of senior executives.

Organisational Planning

For the **Royal Australian Planning Institute** we assisted in the design of a new organisational structure, incorporating the national and state chapters, to maximise services to members.

Workshops

For **BHP** we designed and instigated workshops in the areas of leadership, teamwork, innovation, and behaviour change. These workshops were made accessible for all levels of the business regularly, using pragmatic business concepts.

Customer Service

For **Tint-A-Car** we designed a program focused on customer relationships and the pragmatic business results achieved from the "intangible" components of the business. This allowed the franchisees to refocus their sales and customer service procedures to eliminate costly discounting and price gauging processes thereby increasing profitability significantly without increasing listed pricing.

Assessment & Appraisal

For **New Hope Coal Australia** we assisted the CEO & National HR Manager by interviewing staff on sites for Role Design, Performance Assessment, Salary Appraisal and Psychometric Evaluation. The outcome was a more relevant system of roles & responsibilities ensuring the best fit for people to position, with more equitable remuneration.

"I was fortunate to use the services of Ric here at New Hope Coal. Ric was an invaluable participant in this project as his objective and persuasive argument challenged the thinking of our managers. I was also fortunate to witness Ric's mastery in quickly developing rapport with each of our managers, which is not something I have seen from many other consultants. In addition, while it was not part of his brief, Ric assisted me on a personal development level to understand how to deal with some difficult situations that I face from time to time."

Dianne Armbrust — HR Director, New Hope Coal

Our consulting clients include ...

Giants such as:
- AMP
- Colonial
- Commonwealth Bank
- Ernst & Young
- ExxonMobil
- GE
- Grant Thornton
- HSBC
- Met Life
- Philips Lighting
- PwC
- PT Danamon Bank
- Rider Levett Bucknall
- Siemens
- Suncorp
- Telstra
- Toll
- Westpac

High-growth firms such as:
- Abu Dhabi Gas Liquefaction
- Air Niugini
- Bahrain Petroleum Company
- Bendigo Bank
- Bluescope Steel — Singapore
- Gaby Cool Transport
- Goodman Fielder
- Matilda Fuel Supplies
- Mineral Resources Authority — PNG
- Stockland Property
- Volvo Group Truck

Specialised firms such as:
- CIMB Niaga
- Collex Waste
- Colly Cotton
- DHL
- Hindustan Aeronautics
- Indonesian Aerospace
- Iran Land & Sea
- Jeddah Beverage Can Making
- New Hope Coal
- Red Rooster Foods
- Samsung — Korea
- Snowy Mountain Engineering Corp.
- Subway Restaurants
- Toshiba Corporation — Japan

In the public sector we have worked with organisations such as:
- Australian Public Service Commission
- Department of Parliamentary Services
- Ministry of Finance — Brunei
- Queensland Development & Innovation
- Queensland Health
- Queensland Rail
- Solicitor for the Northern Territory
- Translink

Ric's expertise was all the buzz during my talk and his foundational work in understanding his clients and setting me to leverage his message was truly exceptional. It was a great pleasure to see and work with such a gifted consultant, speaker and writer and I hope I have another chance to do so again. I envy any other professional who gets to work alongside Ric!

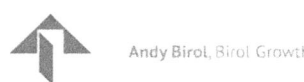

Andy Birol, Birol Growth Consulting

Back to basics recruitment plan

Don't get carried away with all the recruitment tools on the market. Hire for enthusiasm and train for skill, writes **Ric Willmot**

"Unbelievably, the French still use handwriting analysis in hiring, but then again, they drink warm Coca-Cola."

The Russians periodically extract intact from the Siberian ice, those ancient wooly mammoths looking akin to a hairy over-sized elephant.

These specimens are perfectly preserved in time, much like most human resource departments, which seem perfectly preserved in time somewhere around 1970.

The mammoths, of course, are items of special scientific and anthropological interest. HR, unfortunately, we are not so sure about.

Why are we STILL reading about:
- Retention of employees as if they are animals needing to be chained in their cages to keep from escaping
- Four levels of measurement
- Personality profiling and psychometric testing
- Gen Y as if these people are from Jupiter
- Surveys and evaluations

Merely introducing psychometric testing, computerised skill-checks, or (shudder) "electronic online personality profiling" hardly qualifies as modernising HR.

The letters to the editor in these journals seem more concerned about what model of laptop Gen Y employees should be offered than what impact their efforts my have for the employer paying their salaries.

Over the past 20 years, HR has steadily attenuated, to the stage that recruitment is outsourced almost entirely.

Although budgets for training and development remain hefty (most organisations, frankly, prefer simply to throw money at problems than actually grapple with them), HR staffs have been depleted, transactional HR has been outsourced, and transformational HR has become the province of consultants.

And there's a good reason for it: HR is seen as a peripheral function.

HR has to stop focusing on how many male pronouns appear in a procedures and operations manual, whether someone is wearing a perfume to work that is offensive to others, and how many "INFPs" are working in a given department. Instead, HR ought to be focusing on:
- Creating alignment among every position and corporate strategy
- Marrying succession planning to career development and ensuring "bench strength"
- Proactively helping line management with greater efficiencies and productivity
- Optimally focusing resources on the product, the service, and the relationships with customers

Ultimately, HR should disappear completely into the line functions where key managers are held responsible, no less than they are for financial goals or ethical conduct. Ideally, no one should have a career insulated in HR, trapped in the ice until discovered by curious explorers. The mammoths were big, ponderous, and tough.

And they're all dead, every one of them.

Annie Murphy Paul's book, *The Cult of Personality*, demonstrates why most commonly used behavioural assessment and personality "profiling" techniques range from flawed to fraud.

Even the vaunted Rorschach has questionable roots and results. The MBTI (Myers Briggs Type Inventory) has a frighteningly high degree of different results with retesters.

Most of the instruments on the market that are valid (e.g., demonstrate reliability, construct validity, content validity, and concurrent validity) were originally meant to diagnose aberration and mental health problems, not to describe the main, healthy population.

And most of the rest, well, just aren't valid.

You can give a horoscope if you like, and even justify it by saying, "People feel that it does describe them, and I get amazing feedback," but that doesn't make it anything more than a children's guessing game.

I once walked past a manager's office with a large chart on his wall with the 16 MBTI grid clearly displayed with the names of his employees in their assigned box.

His own "type" (I am presuming it was his) was clearly printed on his coffee mug. Who can make this stuff up?

But the war for talent is fiercer than ever with record long-term low unemployment. It is increasingly difficult to discover that 'perfect' candidate.

In days of yore good jobs were jealously sought and difficult to acquire, which meant the hiring corporation was the plenipotentiary of the unemployed and carried ultimate authority in deciding the successful candidate. But as Dylan said, "The times they are a changing."

Employers are continually making compromises, adjustments and trade-offs on skills, aptitude and attitude on a regular basis.

Furthermore, this frequently leads to deficient recruitment decisions; costing the organisation not only money, but time, teamwork, aggravation and inevitably, clients.

Better to know what you are getting yourself into, and how to mitigate the potential downsides, than to be blindsided down the road. If a candidate lacks some required skills, can you hire anyway? Certainly, provided three conditions exist:

1. The candidate really is who she says she is. They applied to a position they are unqualified for, and are trying to convince you they can do it. Be careful they do not get 'too' convincing, and get loose with the truth regarding their qualifications and past performance.
2. And on performance: theirs must be primo. You are already taking a chance on qualifications; do not compound that effort by stretching on diaphanous ability as well. Mediocre applicants? Well wish them the best in their job search.
3. Can the candidate learn? Make sure the candidate is smart enough to learn additional skills, particularly the challenging kind you have been unable to find.

Look for indicators that the person has previously learned on the run.

Importantly, gauge their general desire to work when interviewing and investigating their background.

Submitting new hires to rigorous additional learning while working with veteran skilled professionals and taking on real business challenges will quickly get them the skill they need.

The problems associated with an ever-decreasing talent pool are not going to evaporate along with Australia's water reserves.

Success will reward the informed and astute employers who can hire for enthusiasm and train for skill. It is, however, ironic in this politically correct age of doing somersaults to ensure that no one is offended by a pronoun that we think nothing of providing labels and characterisations to shrugs, moans, and responses to perfectly imperfect instruments.

Unbelievably, the French still use handwriting analysis in hiring, but then again, they drink warm Coca-Cola. ■

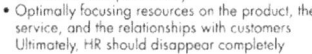

is known as "The Consultant's Consultant" and is dedicated to maximising the profitability of business. You can subscribe to his free monthly e zine, The Executive Times at www.executivewisdom.com

PARTICIPANTS of the four day extensive leadership training paying close attention to consultant Ric Willmot last Thursday. Picture by Mark Talia

CPA workshop helpful to participants

BY MELISHA YAFOI

THE four day intensive executive training that was held in Port Moresby through the Certified Practicing Accountants of PNG in partnership with expert and consultant Ric Willmot was a successful one.

Participant Joap Varap told the *Post-Courier* last Thursday that the training has taught them so many things especially for those who are in the managerial positions.

Mr Varap who is a financial controller with the Monpi Coffee Exports in Goroka said the extensive training has taught them good leadership qualities as well as strategy and change management.

He said the training was educational and important as all the participants deal with people and this is because everyone has different personalities to deal with.

"So the training is more helpful in the sense of giving us a framework not that we use everything that is being given but we use whatever that will be applicable in the organisation.

"One of the things that we can take away with us in terms of change management is to change a person everyday so you're leading a set of team by helping them to change at least 15 per cent of how they are doing things maybe for now or for the year."

He said change cannot happen immediately therefore he has come to understand that as a manager can only change a person at a time and change will eventually take its own toll.

"I am a financial controller but I am also a part of the board of management which making decisions is one of our main thing to do and when you are making decisions it's looking at the company first, if the company doesn't survive, all your people are left without a job so you look at where you going to move forward, I would say cherry on the cake for being in the managerial role," he said.

He said he is pleased with the training and is sure that all the participants will bring back with them something that they will value as managers and directors in their own organisations.

MENTORING & COACHING

For those who want to achieve dramatic professional and business results.

What is unique about my Mentoring & Coaching Program is that it is tailored to each person's individual challenges, context, objectives, and history. The first step is to articulate the objectives, outcomes and results more specifically. This is done from a base of acknowledging the required capabilities and challenges facing the member. The business environment we find ourselves in today is turbulent, complex and uncertain. It necessitates us opening our minds to consider fundamentally diverse ways of perceiving, thinking, leading and living.

Executive coaching has emerged as a critical and valuable tool for supporting executives with these challenges. Our goal as we work together is ultimately to enhance your effectiveness and fulfilment as a professional and as an executive. We will engage in a purposeful dialogue of development and reflection to expand perspectives and insights, explore the robustness of thinking as a skill, and generate new possibilities for action. My approach draws upon personal experience in the business and consulting arenas combined with methodologies from systems thinking and organisational psychology. Be aware that the executive coaching & mentoring we do together does not distinguish between or treat separately, work from home. You are a whole person.

The Process

Executive coaching & mentoring is a partnership that is successful when based on the power of trust. There will be the occasion where the learning is challenging and may result in discoveries about the way your actions, thoughts and feelings play a part in creating obstacles that you may need to overcome. Some members have at times been uncomfortable with the experience as they are stretched into a new and unfamiliar territory. The member's willingness to invite and welcome these points of discomfort allow them to increase capacity to exercise new learning and grow developmentally.

The coaching relationship will at times be highly energised, and at other times will experience emotional lows or test points when challenges arise, and doubt or resistance shows up. There is an ongoing evaluation of the effectiveness of the process, and we require the commitment and willingness of the member to go with us to the edge of their learning limits. My task is to create the conditions for reflective learning by providing a space that allows the member to take stock and observe themselves about their challenges.

> *Ric is very engaging and has been an inspiration to me. His practical, no-nonsense approach to resolving issues is tailored specifically to help me with my personal development. My sessions with Ric are always very focused and never once have I found my mind wandering. I always feel inspired, empowered and keen to apply the ideas we discussed.*

Huang Meng Lee, PWC

The Objective

The initial phase is to clarify and establish the objectives, outcomes and results the member desires and to develop a coaching & mentoring relationship. This is akin to a discovery process in specifically determining the needs and expectations along with the coaching framework that will be used. These objectives may alter as the member develops increasing awareness of their capabilities, challenges and new opportunities, over time. This also provides for increased growth and development as it caters for the fact that each person's learning outcomes and intentions are not static. Overall, the initial phase sets the foundation for the coaching & mentoring relationship. It establishes rapport, determines the context and lays out the best way to work together and support the learning.

Your History

There is a significant challenge where there is no shared history between the member and me. To obtain a baseline picture and to increase the member's self-awareness for articulating the personal intentions and development, an assessment may be needed. Not all assessments will be undertaken at the outset of the executive coaching & mentoring program. What data is sourced, whom the member would like to involve, how we source data and eventually use it will all be dependent on the key learnings and insights that emerge from the Program.

The assessment may take on various forms:

- A structured psychological evaluation incorporating measures of preference, life and career anchors, leadership archetypes and style, leadership competencies, mental functioning, and other characteristics.
- Powerful questions to serve as reflection frameworks for the member to gather their own insights and data about things that matter to them.
- 360-Degree feedback data – both structured and self-directed to obtain more insight from key people in the member's life and work.
- If applicable, the superior's view on the member's progress can also be solicited as important assessment data at key points.

The Program

The executive coaching & mentoring will vary in intensity and content depending on the objectives and needs of the member. The effectiveness of the Program will be subject to ongoing review. We monitor the member's progress against the agreed development plan and the key intentions they set for themselves which we will formulate, review and update throughout the executive coaching & mentoring program. The member may be required to augment the coaching & mentoring by undertaking:

- Action learning assignments
- Challenges as set down by me
- Role plays, readings, journaling
- Shadowing

There are some matters that are sacrosanct:

- Confidentiality
- Understanding and appreciating my role and the accountability of the member
- Determining with clarity the needs of the member
- Understanding the organisational context in which these requirements are placed
- Appreciating preferred learning processes and sequences
- Agreement regarding logistics

Indicatively, most Managing Director, Board Director, Owner, or C-Level executive coaching & mentoring takes the form of a two-hour- face-to-face session, twice per month over an initial period of nine to twelve months. This time frame allows for the internalisation of outcomes which are more transformational in nature. At the scheduled end of the program, the member's progress is formally reviewed and a sign-off done on the enhancements achieved. At this point, the coaching & mentoring relationship might be terminated or phased out over a series of sessions, or an additional program with new, revised or extended objectives, outcomes and results may be enacted.

> *Ric does not let me accept 2nd best for myself and pushes me to strive forward in his own tactful manner. After spending time with Ric I have my perspective back where it should be and viewing issues with an honest and real viewpoint.*

Michelle Gaby, Gaby Cool Transport

Individual Mentor Program

Six months of coaching & mentoring with **unlimited access** to Ric Willmot via telephone, fax, e-mail, and video-conferencing.

Target Mentor Program

Six, nine, or twelve months of **unlimited access** to Ric Willmot and a structured (guided) approach to achieve pre-set targets with you being accountable for milestones.

Retainer Program

Twelve (or nine) months executive coaching & mentoring with Ric Willmot that includes regular two-hour face-to-face meetings as well as **unlimited access** via telephone, fax, e-mail, and video-conferencing.

Commercials & Logistics

There are some variations available in joining the program. These options allow the member to determine how to gain the best guidance within the limits of their resources (time, geographic locale, access, and investment). The choice also depends on the complexity of the role the member holds and the issues to be addressed. Options include but are not limited to:

- Hourly coaching rates
- Monthly fixed-fee
- 6-month program fixed-fee
- 9 & 12-month retainers

Because Executive Wisdom Consulting works across geographic boundaries, all amounts quoted exclude any applicable GST or VAT. The prices are in US Dollars. The investment quoted excludes costs associated with any psychometric or other third party assessment material that we may decide to use. Senior executives who join a *Target Edition* or use the *Retainer Option* will be liable for any mutually agreed travel[1] and accommodation expenses deemed necessary.

Retainers range from $0 - $10,000 per month and the programs range from $1,500 - $125,000.

Hourly rates arranged by agreement.

To discuss options for you or your organisation, contact Ric Willmot directly by sending a Callback Request SMS message to his telephone: +61 412.728-113 or an e-mail to ric@mba4day.com

---

Thanks so much for your help. I have covered my 12-month investment in your services after just 2 weeks.

   **Mark Jocumsen**, Better Business Outcomes

---

[1] All domestic air travel is business class, and even though we choose to fly first class internationally, you will be invoiced for business class fares only.

To whom are we listening?

Don't look for 'yes' men to tell you it's all okay. Challenge and be challenged to achieve great things, writes **Ric Willmot**.

Through my travels this month, I have had the pleasure of speaking with people from my Mentor Program who described to me:

Significant increases in business owing to fervently making a stand on fee levels and arduous negotiating; improved and increased acceptance ratios on business proposals because of strong value expressions and options to achieve results; expansion and augmentation of contracts with existing clients that resulted in six-figure engagements over several years; introduction of products and remote services creating passive income for the first time; and scheduling of three or more vacation trips for 2007 with the intent of scheduling work around them and the observance of that time as sacrosanct.

Why am I telling you this? Because I have also heard people tell me that they "can't" and that they "don't see how it can be done".

One person said, "This is all really cerebral, isn't it?".

Yes. Assuming you have the aptitude, capacity and forte to accomplish your goals, or can develop those traits, skills and talent, it's all about your self-discipline. I am not meaning the stupid mental affirmations that the guests on Oprah declaim as the route to Nirvana ("I CAN do it, I CAN do it!"), but rather the mental set that has you plan, prepare, deliver, follow-up, learn from mistakes, refine, and improve.

Don't surround yourself with people who are "supportive" and tell you it's "alright" that you feel the way you do or that you're not doing better than you are. Surround yourself with people who will kick your backside to breakfast for not trying harder. Commiseration is insidious; competition is invigorating.

To whom are we listening? Who are we using as our exemplars and role models? From whom have we decided to accept advice? These are all voluntary choices, yet we seem to have them often foisted upon us, unchallenged, and wholly swallowed.

Because Oprah Winfrey has more money than most European countries, does that qualify her to use the media to broadcast her choices of current books and thereby accelerate their sales? She wields immense power, and makes "hits" out of airheads. But Oprah often puts people on "display," and makes jokes at their expense. Her behaviour with that fraudulent novelist was reprehensible: Back him blindly until the public turned on her, then make a deal to have him come on her show, humiliate him, and add still more to his book sales, and show the public she's "learned." Please!

Bertrand Russell said once, "Don't ever be absolutely sure of anything — not even if I tell you". I've learned a great deal from "unknowns" and through casual meetings. I've been bored, and sometimes enraged, by those who are extolled as "experts." It's not because I'm a contrarian, but simply because I refuse to dive into the mainstream without checking the current and looking for rocks. Predetermined, premeditated, premature solutions have no inherent value. There are four basic patterns of thinking about your business and career:

1. What's going on? Get clarification and look objectively at the strategy you have operating currently.
2. Why is the business the way it is? The cause-and-effect analysis. Accumulate the knowledge you require to be even more successful than you currently are. Move beyond mere reaction to the environment, to make use of the environment.
3. Which course of action should you take? Allow for choice and give yourself options!
4. What lies ahead? What might be the future? Test arguments and philosophies, and search for positive instances as well as counter examples with critical thinking.

Someone asked me why a certain successful person occasionally visits me to have lunch, when he knows I'm going to relentlessly demonstrate what he's still missing.

The reason is that he's smart enough not to believe his own media, not to assume that his present station in life is the end of the line, and not to stop reaching.

Life is short and careers shorter. How many consecutive days are you willing to tell yourself that you can't do something or don't want to try something? How many weeks can you perpetuate the self-created myth that you can't afford professional development or that the time isn't right? How many months can you tolerate being on a plateau that will eventually erode?

Just making people "feel better" is insufficient, especially if there is no actual improvement.

Chicken Soup for the Soul has sold millions, Oprah has millions of viewers, and pet rocks sold in the millions; that does not make them worthwhile. Men are from Mars, women are from Venus, and people who believe that are from Jupiter. Set your own strategy instead of following the herd. Surround yourself with people and experiences which will help you grow, not coddle you. Bathe in success, not complacency. Because you need a fresh flow of water, not a stagnant pond. ■

Willmot, Ric, known as "The Consultant's Consultant" is the CEO of Executive Wisdom Consulting Group, www.executivewisdom.com and the founder of the Society for Executive Wisdom, www.executivewisdomsociety.com

MANAGEMENT RESOURCES GUIDE

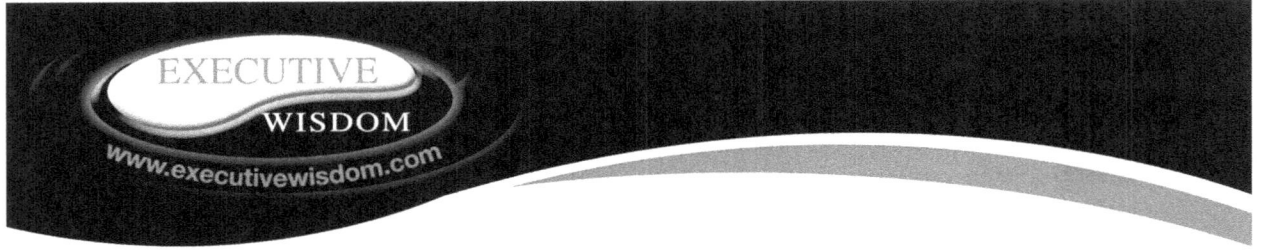

Finding a Critical Friend

A Reason and Framework for Executive Coaching

Ric Willmot

Executive Wisdom Consulting Group Pty Ltd
Willbert House 68 Mayfield Road, Carina Qld 4152 Australia
PO Box 44 Carina Qld 4152 Australia
T: +61 7 3395 1050 F: +61 7 3395 1805 E: info@executivewisdom.com
Los Angeles Office Telephone: +1 213-985-3395

Finding a Critical Friend

If you are trying to create a new way to be for yourself or your organization, you will often become painfully aware of just how far away you are from your goals. This can be emotionally wrenching, especially during the inevitable stages where you meet resistance, hostility, and delays in the system. This is particularly the case for executives finding their way in a new role or wishing to change fundamentally the role they currently occupy.

The ideal strategy is to move gently, continually toward your vision for the organization, learning to live with the feelings of stress and emotional tension. But it's not easy, and all the conventional strategies for dealing with that tension make matters worse. Executives faced with disappointment force themselves to 'push harder'; they lower their vision ("We don't really need to make this reform complete"), or they deny that they have any emotional tension at all, for fear of burdening the organization ("Current reality is not so bad.").

Any of these strategies will undermine your purpose. If only as a safety valve to preserve your change effort, you need to find a way to cultivate awareness of your own emotional tension, without giving in to it. You need to make sure you are taking care of yourself and you need to find ways to face your own patterns and ways of dealing with people honestly and squarely.

Some people claim that they can go off and meditate by themselves and clear the emotional tension they feel. But for most people in organizations, a better strategy is to find a partner whom they can trust. Leaders, regardless of "rank," need a partner and critical friend to talk to and confide in while going through the often intense phases of change.

This is particularly so for executives for they are likely to be the recipients of the most inauthentic communication in any organization. Whatever is presented to them is always highly filtered data and meanings and they tend to feel that many who work for them cannot also be critical of them.

Why is the presence of this partner and critical friend so important? Because if you are the leader, the rest of the people on your team or in your organization expect to see you project openness and honesty – including the confidence to say what you believe in, and to admit when you are uncertain. They expect you to be effective and flexible in your social dealings with them and others, and they expect you to have a much higher level of sensitivity and concern (both at a systems level and interpersonally) than you will often consider yourself capable of delivering.

It is much easier to pull this off if you are in steady contact with someone who can help you uncover what you are thinking and feeling, including your misgivings, who can help you reframe your understanding of what is actually going on (and your part in it) and who without fear or favour will tell you "the way it is".

Executive Wisdom Consulting Group Pty Ltd
Willbert House 68 Mayfield Road, Carina Qld 4152 Australia
PO Box 44 Carina Qld 4152 Australia
T: +61 7 3395 1050 F: +61 7 3395 1805 E: info@executivewisdom.com
Los Angeles Office Telephone: +1 213-985-3395

Critical friends may have a vision of your potential, but they thoroughly accept you as you are now. They may be people you pay for the time they spend with you doing this "work" or they may already be someone you know. If you contract someone for this service, they become as it were an "Executive Coach" to and for you. But their fee, their experience, their skill and their qualifications will count for naught unless they are people who are there for you, both as person and in your new found role.

As you sort through the people and professionals in your life, you may discover that only one or two people meet these criteria – and your significant other or spouse may not be one of them. They have other important roles to fill in your life!

This is a different dynamic from finding a sympathetic person on whom you can "dump" your bad feeling when you get away from work. In systems terms, when you "dump," you're shifting the burden of your feelings onto the dumpee. If you generate strong emotional tension at work, and take it home and spill it onto a friend or spouse, there's a cathartic release and the tension goes out of your system.

Then you are ready to go back and build up more negative tension, while your friend or spouse copes with the fact that you have used him or her, once again, as a repository vessel for your negative feelings.

On the other hand, when you find a worthy partner and critical friend associated with work, you are designing a more fundamental solution, in which the tension is named, witnessed, and used as energy to influence the system at work. Your goal is to forge an alliance, or create some form of mutual commitment, in which there is trust and freedom of expression. Make a point of allowing your prospective partner and critical friend to make an informed choice about taking on the role. Describe the changes you see ahead and make your expectations clear; ask if he or she is willing to serve as a sounding board, colleague, and personal consultant, i.e. an executive coach.

Given the current reality of the organization where you work, you will probably find it difficult to imagine having this kind of partnership. It is more likely you will need to build it outside the organization. And it will be helpful in the long term to you if the person you choose has strengths, experiences and insights in those areas that are your blind-spots.

In a good "partner and critical friend" conversation you can blow off steam without the burden of having to follow through. You may end up expressing your emotional tension in words, gestures, tears, or angry shouting – that's part of the process. Your partner and critical friend may surprise you sometimes by saying something like: "I can see it's worse than you're letting on. You're deeply hurt." There is a moment of great release and awareness when you recognize that someone else has articulated what you've felt below the surface.

Executive Wisdom Consulting Group Pty Ltd
Willbert House 68 Mayfield Road, Carina Qld 4152 Australia
PO Box 44 Carina Qld 4152 Australia
T: +61 7 3395 1050 F: +61 7 3395 1805 E: info@executivewisdom.com
Los Angeles Office Telephone: +1 213-985-3395

A "partner and critical friend" conversation will also remind you that while your feelings are absolutely legitimate, they may also change soon; your commitment, is to the truth as you see it each moment, not to consistency.

A "partner and critical friend" conversation will often involve diagrams, doodling, sketches and frameworks new to you as you learn to see your problems and concerns from different angles, different perspectives and build new insights as to how to act. It will be a safe and psychological space in which you can learn and grow.

Always let your partner and critical friend know how you would like her or him to listen at any particular meeting or on any particular day. Partners and critical friends may listen only as a sounding board, with no verbal response but lots of emotional response. They may listen and offer responses that show you how others will perceive your comments later. They may advise on strategies and tactics, or offer more wide-ranging insights.

Whatever form they take, these conversations are a sort of transformer, temporarily adding capacity to your emotional circuits. That is why your partner and critical friend will not help you much by telling you how the other people in your team feel about the situation, or how "it does you no good to be angry." People need a partner and critical friend precisely because they need help seeing their feelings, looking at their responses, uncovering the consequences of their actions, both intended and unintended.

Similarly, it doesn't help to have someone say: "If you're feeling so angry, what are you going to do about it?" There is a profound difference between the actions that you might take when driven by the desire to reduce your emotional tension, and the strategic actions that will emerge after the tension has been transformed into positive creative energy.

Eventually, your partner and critical friend will probably be the first to recognize the point when the organization and you are more than halfway planted in its new reality. Both of you can construct questions or metrics to test the assumption that your organization and/or you have indeed "turned the corner." Once you have evidence, you can do for your organization what your partner and critical friend has done for you - point to the light at the end of the tunnel.

So, now, as you have read these notes, you are coming to a point where you can start to make some choices: will your partner and critical friend be someone with whom you already are friends? Or, will they be someone else: although contracted by you, someone whose integrity and way of being in the world you trust, whom you contract with for a certain regular time: an executive coach.

We wish you well in this choice and in your role!

For further information contact Ric Willmot

Executive Wisdom Consulting Group Pty Ltd
Willbert House 68 Mayfield Road, Carina Qld 4152 Australia
PO Box 44 Carina Qld 4152 Australia
T: +61 7 3395 1050 F: +61 7 3395 1805 E: info@executivewisdom.com
Los Angeles Office Telephone: +1 213-985-3395

Ric Willmot
Executive Wisdom Consulting Group

It is with pleasure that I am able to write this testimonial for Ric Willmot.

I first met Ric some six years ago as he MC'd and presented at two separate MEA (Meeting and Events Australia) conferences. Armed with his customised presentation and impeccable manners, he captured the attention of room full of noisy, know-it-all sales people and turned on a light (or three) in every recharged mind. Having been in the hospitality sales industry for many years, it was refreshing to engage a professional speaker/presenter who could stretch the imagination of a (sometime know-it-all) profession into thinking outside the square.

Having changed roles now and putting the shoe on the other foot in representing the "talent", I have seen the other side of Ric Willmot. To sum Ric up in two words, I would use Loyal and Honest. Loyal because he will stand by the "agent" and work along side them to win the piece of business – going that extra mile! And because he will stand by the "client" from the moment of introduction and to offer continuous support and counselling after the event. Honest because he has an open communication between the client and himself, and always keeping the agent in the loop.

Ric's expertise and background allow him to confidently give straight forward advice even to industry colleagues that enable us to do what we do well.

In closing I would like to also admire and recognize the extra effort that Ric puts in; he goes beyond the scope of his engagement to ensure his client and agent receive value for money and ensure they act on it to receive the benefit.

I would not hesitate to recommend any client or agent to work with Ric; from initial contact he will ensure all parties are prepared and makes sure resources are available.

If you require any further clarification or would like to discuss personally, please do not hesitate to contact me.

Kind Regards

Melanie Williamson
Onstage Entertainment

PROFESSIONAL SPEAKING

In his presentations, Ric shares easy-to-implement, proven strategies that have a profound effect on his audience and encourages the attendees to execute ideas that make a positive difference. Ric delivers substance that is relevant to the real world of business, and the challenges businesspeople confront. His presentations are replete with relevance, evidence, wisdom, and amusing anecdotes to ensure that every member of the audience will take away time-proven strategies for long-lived success. He achieves this by taking the time to craft a customised presentation that is filled with substance, strategies and solutions that your delegates can apply to their jobs and their lives. His strategies are not out-of-date clichés. They are sustainable, bottom-line enhancing, performance ideas that do work. Ric is a unique, entertaining and an authoritative speaker who uses every means available to make his message memorable, practical, and powerful.

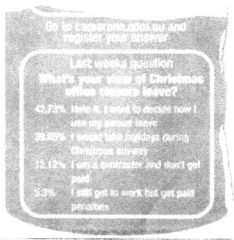

▶ PEOPLE

Dawes herself initiated and drove the tender process through which the Prop House recently won a three-year contract as the Turf Club's preferred theming and linen supplier for major race day events, including the Melbourne Cup.

This will earn the company $200,000 a year, with much of that turnover coming in historically quiet periods.

Nervous about change, Dawes is nevertheless excited about her new role (there's also the bonus of not working all those hours, a boon to a sleep-deprived new mother).

As Dawes steps back from the internal workings of her business, a traditionally loose company structure will tighten up.

The formalised reporting system that will keep Dawes informed through her COO will be duplicated throughout the company.

Key Prop House employees will take on added responsibilities as roles and lines of communication become more clearly defined.

"I guess now the business revolves more around the positions that the business needs to keep running and at the moment it's fantastic, I've got the people to fill those positions — but the positions are there," Dawes says.

"I've always been a bit of an open door policy person — which I still am — but I think to put those really strong lines of communication in place gives everyone clear direction as to where they need to report to."

While redoing "the org chart" was her idea, having an independent business consultant on board was important to the process, says Dawes.

"Sometimes when you work so closely within a business, you can become a little bit blind and a little bit precious," she says.

"So it's been really handy having an outsider to clarify everything for me — and also to help by coming in and talking to the staff individually to find out what they feel the business is lacking or where it can improve."

> "As a business owner, it's really difficult; I could easily be working 24-7 and still not get everything done."

"Together we've moulded this whole new organisational structure and a way of moving forward and growing the business."

The hard part for Dawes — a self-described "control freak" — will be making sure she herself adheres to the new structure.

"I've got to really keep an eye on myself, that I don't start upsetting the apple cart by jumping over people that I've put in place for a reason.

"It's a waste of time if I come back after 10 months of having the baby and take over again; that's a waste, it won't be going anywhere."

In fact, Dawes says these changes are long overdue and the only way for the company to move forward.

While the new structure would have worked just as well a year ago, impending motherhood gave her the "push" she needed to finally put it in place, she says.

Dawes has been mindful of setting attainable financial goals over the coming transition period, so as not to put the company under undue pressure (the goals for this year are a 12 percent increase in sales and one more major client contract of two-plus years).

That said, she expects clearer structure and direction to reap rewards as a matter of course.

To business owners who — for whatever reason — are contemplating taking a step back from their operations while retaining a meaningful over-arching role, Dawes has this advice: make sure you're ready.

"If you're not really ready to do it, you're not going to do it properly," she says.

"And once you make that decision and provided you find the right person or people to take over, let them do it.

"Let them do what you want them to do because that's going to allow you to do what ultimately you want to do." ■

Chefs, shrinks and thieves

Trust in yourself, be convinced of your own value, and aim to be successful rather than perfect, writes **Ric Willmot**.

The All Ordinaries here in Australia is over 5,800 and continuing to approach 6,000. The Dow Jones in the United States has broken 12,000.

Does anyone want to make a case that success in this economy is dependent on anything other than discipline, action and common sense? I am weary of pessimism as an excuse for non-performance.

When have you been greeted, in a prestigious restaurant, by the chef, welcoming you but warning, "I am really not that good, and there are better equipped kitchens, and if you've got any suggestions, I can alter my cooking styles and methods"?

Great restaurants, where reservations can be difficult to get, make it known that they have the best food anywhere, the chef has pop-star status, and even take a dim view of any substitutions requested by diners.

We all implicitly trust these chefs, at least the first time, because you are hoping they know more than you do and possess unique cooking talents and recipes. Moreover, no one attempts to bargain about the price.

Why then, do consultants, accountants, lawyers and other professional services businesspeople, so easily lose their nerve when they are approached by (or they approach) prospective clients. I have actually heard an accountant state that they couldn't calculate the invoice for the client until they had subtracted 'write-offs.' The client had never implied, at any stage during the meeting, that he was concerned about the fees.

A lawyer discussing an acquisition project said to a member of my Mentor Program, "The fee is $30,000, but if that's too much, there are ways to reduce it." This is an attitudinal challenge. The recipe for success is that we must understand, appreciate and be convinced of our own value.

1. Identify the value that you deliver for your clients, to improve their condition.
2. Ensure that you are passionate about this value offering.
3. Then persistently keep acquiring the proficiency to escalate and dispense that value.

If you have those skills, you will never be intimidated and you will always serve a great meal.

Some years ago, I wrote an article stating that failures in professional services businesses were due mainly to lack of capital. I am now convinced that the leading cause of failure is a lack of self-esteem. They do not believe their own value proposition and thereby don't believe they are really worth higher fees, and do not consider themselves as peers of the client.

Psychologists, unfairly, have a reputation for taking a patient's mild anxiety and turning it into stark raving fear. Nevertheless, over a luncheon conference, a psychologist provided me with the best piece of advice I have ever received, "It's not about perfection, it's about success".

We continually strive for 'perfection,' when we only need to 'succeed' at our professional endeavours. The horse finishing first wins 10 times the purse of the second place mount, but only needs to be in front by a nose.

The winner of a golf tournament doesn't need to shoot a perfect game, but rather be just one stroke ahead of the next best at the end of four rounds. So, to increase our chances of success, how can we build self-esteem?

1. **Formalise your strength inventory.**
   What have you really excelled at in your profession, and cite the evidence? When you have your list, study it, appreciate yourself for achieving it, and then brand it.

2. **Broaden your vocabulary.**
   Improve your grammar, and you will stand out in a crowd.

3. **Don't fear failure.**
   To quote Winston Churchill, "Success is not final, failure is not fatal; it is the courage to continue is what counts".

4. **Network with challenging people, who are smarter, more successful and more travelled than you.**
   Learn to be comfortable with them, ask intelligent questions, and challenge unsubstantiated statements. If you can do it socially, you can do it professionally.

5. **Learn social graces and best etiquette.**
   There's not enough being taught in our schools any more.

Estimates are that 1.5 exabytes (1.5×10^{18}) of unique information will be generated worldwide this year. That's estimated to be more than in the previous 5,000 years.

The amount of new technical information is doubling every two years. For students starting a four-year technical or college degree, this means that half of what they learn in their first year of study will be outdated by their third year of study. It is predicted to double every 72 hours by 2010.

All this technical knowledge comes at price sometimes, and significantly, the cost has included at varying degrees, 'common sense.' When asked why he robbed banks, Willy Sutton replied, "Because that is where the money is".

Yet, there is a preponderance of fallowed marketing efforts by professional services. None of us drives the freeways with the purpose of reading advertising billboards, and I know of no one who enjoys telephone solicitations or cold calls. So why would we consider these as successful marketing strategies to build our own businesses?

It is better to have clients coming to you, stating they have heard of you, and wondered how you might be able to help them. This happens when you have built a brand. Like Willy, you need to position yourself where the money is. Identify clearly who your target audience is for your services. Then you will know where to network, because you know where they hang out. You will know where to advertise or have articles published, because you know what they read. You will know what association meetings to attend or speak at, because you will know where they are members.

Your brand must be distinctive, and the benefits to your customers have to be functional, but importantly must also tap into the visceral needs. Behind every corporate objective is a personal objective! Finally, your brand has to be congruent with your competencies, real and perceived.

I don't want a theorist telling me how to scuba dive the Barrier Reef, because I might just get the bends, or drown. I want someone who has dived down that particular reef with expertise and success. You don't want to follow the advice of someone who describes how to make Lobster Thermidor. You want someone who can cook. ■

> **Willmot,**
> Ric, known as "The Consultant's Consultant," is the CEO of Executive Wisdom Consulting Group; a consultancy that improves the effectiveness of organisations through impossible thinking.

BONUS MATERIALS

BONUS MATERIALS FOR YOU TO USE

Understanding the Myers-Briggs Grid

The Myers-Briggs instrument is a worthwhile and valuable tool. My opinion is that it has been corrupted and devalued by egregious individuals and organisations who have manipulated the marketplace into believing it does more than what it can or was ever supposed to do. It has in some corporate circles become a holy grail of recruiting and managing people, which is wrong and dangerous, as well as disrespectful to the psychological profession. It should NEVER under any circumstances be used as a tool to determine the appropriateness of job candidates, promotions, leadership determinations, and the like. That being said, many people ask me to give them a simple snapshot of each of the sixteen types. It is likely because 99% of the people selling MBTI as a training resource do not understand it and have never been properly trained in any event. This chart is thanks to Tim Dalmau.

ISTJ	ISFJ	INFJ	INTJ
Natural Organiser	Practical Solutions	Inspiring Leaders	Results Matter
ISTP	ISFP	INFP	INTP
Quiet Achiever	Actions speak louder than words	Care for people	Creative Thinkers
ESTP	ESFP	ENFP	ENTP
Just do it	Let's have fun	People are the product	Process is the product
ESTJ	ESFJ	ENFJ	ENTJ
Natural Administrator	Everybody's friend	Smooth persuader	Natural commander

If you would like to introduce the genuine value of what appropriate Psychometric Tools can deliver in your organisation contact us:

E: ric@mba4day.com

T: +61 7 3395 1050

Send a text message to +61 412 728 113 for a personal callback by Ric Willmot

© Ric Willmot 2004

MANAGEMENT RESOURCES GUIDE

DIAGNOSTIC GUIDE

Tools for Hearing the Customer — How to audit your business communications

Diagnostic spreadsheet to assist in auditing business communications to convert general interest into new business.

TOOL	NATURE & PURPOSE	ADVANTAGES	DISADVANTAGES
FOCUS GROUP	Small groups (of customers or any target group) are invited to meet with a facilitator to answer open-ended questions.	The technique found most useful in research. It gives an intimate view of customers and allows them to provide information they wouldn't mention in surveys.	A small group of customers may not adequately represent your total customer base.
CUSTOMER PANEL	Similar to a focus group, a customer panel consists of a small number of customers invited to answer open-ended questions. However, this group meets on a regular basis.	Regular meetings create even greater intimacy than focus groups. Customers who think about your problems over the long term may come up with especially good ideas.	Customer panels require considerable management effort.
FACE-TO-FACE INTERVIEW	Personal interviews provide nuances of different customers' thoughts.	In groups, customers influence one another's responses. Individual interviews enable customers to articulate more idiosyncratic thoughts.	In groups, customers help each other articulate thoughts that may not be clear at first. In individual interviews, you lose that.
CUSTOMER VISIT AND OBSERVATION OF THEIR PRODUCT USE	A thoughtful study of customers in the setting in which they use your product presumably provides the greatest intimacy of any technique.	The most under-utilised method. When people who know what the product is designed to do, see how people use it, they form ideas for improvement that customers themselves could never have proposed.	This method has fewer disadvantages than you'd expect. Many customers are delighted to be visited. Visits, however, require planning. Establish a systematic plan of what you're looking for before your visit.
CUSTOMER TOUR	Invite customers to visit your facilities and discuss how you can serve them better.	Customers offer excellent ideas whilst at your site.	Tours won't provide a comprehensive understanding of customer views.
TRADE SHOW MEETING	Having a booth in a place where customers will congregate is a cost-effective, as well as time-honoured method of hearing the customer.	You can meet more customers per dollar expended than with other methods.	There is little time to talk privately, and the atmosphere is artificial.
TOLL-FREE TELEPHONE	Companies attach telephone numbers to products or their literature.	An effective method of gathering data from customers when problems are being experienced. It also improves satisfaction and generates add-on sales.	Can be expensive.
SURVEY — TELEPHONE OR ONLINE	A menu of static questions asked of a vast number of people. They're most useful to obtain opinions on closed questions, the importance of which is established by asking open-ended questions in other settings.	If well managed, they can provide scientifically valid information on what customers think. (Meetings in small groups cannot reliably represent what the entire customer base thinks.)	You will obtain little information on anything other than the specific questions you ask. (The question, "Do you have other suggestions?" seldom produces profound responses.)
MYSTERY SHOPPER	Professionals visit your business posing as customers and report on how they are treated.	Provides accurate information on the service you offer.	May cause employees to feel they are not trusted.
DEBRIEFING OF FRONTLINE STAFF	Ask frontline people in a relaxed setting about their experiences to obtain insight into what the customer faces and wants.	This method taps the vast pool of data your organisation already possesses.	This is not a complete solution, but has little downside risk.
CUSTOMER CONTACT LOG	Ask customer contact people to report when customers say something interesting or significant.	Capture data from the place that many customers are initially likely to go first with a problem.	Frontline staff perceives "customer contact reports" as a bureaucratic nuisance. You must evaluate the quality of information and show you're acting on the data if you are to receive useful information.
CUSTOMER SERVICE PERSON'S HOTLINE	A phone number that customer service people call to report problems. A voicemail may be sufficient.	A hotline not only provides information, but gives an extra sense of power to the frontline staff.	Data must be managed carefully to be useful.
COMPETITIVE WIN/LOSS DEBRIEFING	These are special interviews with the customer at the time you win or lose a piece of business.	Taken at a time when the customer has had time thinking through their most pressing needs and comparing you to competitors. Helps significantly when conducted by an objective party.	The customer may not wish to participate honestly.

+61 7 3395 1050 ric@mba4day.com
+61 7 3395 1805 www.mba4day.com
Willbert House 68 Mayfield Road Carina QLD, Australia 4152

 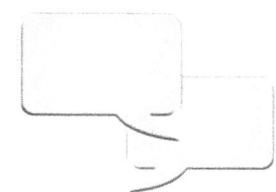

BEST PRACTICE GUIDE

Transforming from Crisis Management to Crisis Leadership

In September 1982 Tylenol capsules laced with potassium cyanide killed seven people in the Chicago area and is a case study for crisis management. Although much has been learned since, many organisations still have not adopted proactive crisis leadership programs. Until organisations do so, they will be crisis-prone, susceptible to an ever-growing number of crises.

Crisis management is no longer sufficient. In this modern era, where technology, data, information, manufacturing, etc., is ever-increasing as exponentially faster rates, crisis leadership is critical. The difference between the two is the crisis leadership is directional: crisis management is reactive, responding to crises after they had occurred. In contrast, crisis leadership is proactive, seeking to plan for crises that eventuate. Crisis management tends to consider individual crises in isolation, while crisis leadership considers the big picture—how individual crises interact. Unless your organisation takes position of crisis leadership, you cannot respond properly when a crisis occurs. Intelligent leaders anticipate the broadest possible range of potential concerns.

7 Pillars of Crises

It can be generalized that there are seven pillars or categories to which crises belong:

1. Economic
2. Informational
3. Physical
4. Human resources
5. Reputational
6. Psychopathic acts
7. Natural disasters

Understanding these pillars provides insights to ten key lessons that crisis-prepared organisations have learned that are helpful to use as a template for organisations developing crisis leadership:

1) Prepare for at least one crisis under each pillar.
2) It is not sufficient to prepare only for industry-specific crises.
3) Prepare for the simultaneous occurrence of multiple crises.
4) The purpose of definitions is to guide, not predict.
5) Every type of crisis can happen to every organisation.
6) No type of crisis should be taken literally.
7) Tampering is the most generic form or type of all crises.
8) No crisis ever happens in the precise way you plan for it, so it's not crisis planning per se that's important, it's thinking about the unthinkable.
9) Every crisis is capable of being both the cause and the effect of any other crisis.
10) Crisis leadership is systemic.

BEST PRACTICE GUIDE

Transforming from Crisis Management to Crisis Leadership   .../2

Crisis Pillar	Examples
Economic	Labour strikes
	Labour unrest
	Labour shortage
	Major decline in stock price and price fluctuations
	Market crash
	Decline in major earnings
Informational	Loss of proprietary and confidential information
	False information
	Tampering with computer records
	Tampering with cloud data
	Loss of key information regarding customers, suppliers, etc.
Physical (loss of key plants or facilities)	Loss of key equipment, plants, and material supplies
	Breakdown of key equipment, plants, etc.
	Loss of key facilities
	Major plant disruptions
Human resources	Loss of key executives
	Loss of key personnel
	Rise in absenteeism
	Rise in workplace accidents
	Rise in vandalism
	Workplace violence, harassment, etc.
Reputational	Slander and gossip
	Rumours
	Damage to corporate reputation
	Tampering with corporate branding and marketing collateral
	Social media attacks
Psychopathic acts	Product tampering
	Kidnapping
	Hostage-taking
	Terrorism
	Workplace violence
Natural Disasters	Earthquakes
	Floods/Typhoons/Hurricanes/Cyclones/Tsunamis
	Fires/Explosions
	Droughts

+61 7 3395 1050   ric@mba4day.com
+61 7 3395 1805   www.mba4day.com
Willbert House 68 Mayfield Road Carina QLD, Australia 4152

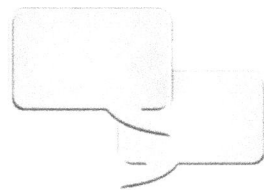

BEST PRACTICE GUIDE

Transforming from Crisis Management to Crisis Leadership   .../3

> *"You need to plan the way a fire department plans; capable of responding to the unanticipated as well as to any ordinary event."* — Andrew Grove

Making it Happen

- Assemble and train a cross-functional, cross-divisional crisis team.
- Poll individual members of the team with regard to the crises they can envision because of their distinct vantage points.
- Produce three to five general maps or big pictures showing how each of the individual crises that the various team members envision might interact so as to set off a chain reaction.
- Referring to the overall maps, determine what pieces of data can be used as early warning signals to announce the beginning stages of each individual crisis and indicate the likelihood that it will set off a chain reaction of other crises.

Become conversant with the seven pillars and the ten key lessons. Look for patterns and interconnections. The creation of visual maps is one of the best tools your organisation can develop. Crisis leadership must not only be embraced, but it must be done exceptionally well. You don't want your organisation to be the next Tylenol.

Bring the best executive and management learning to your organisation by having the 4-Day MBA delivered in-house. Contact us to arrange a telephone appointment to discuss your options and the opportunities that can be created for the development of your management team.

E: ric@mba4day.com
Send a text message to: +61 412 728 113 for a callback.

Management Training Needs Request

How far into the future does this assessment incorporate planning needs? ☑
- 6 months ☐
- 12 months ☐
- 18 months ☐
- 24 months ☐
- 30 months ☐
- 36 months ☐

When do you hope to do this training (month/year)? _____

Nominate the required topics for management training ☑

- Business Thinking ☐
- CEO Thinking ☐
- Change/Transformation ☐
- Coaching & Mentoring ☐
- Communication Skills ☐
- Conflict Management ☐
- Culture Change ☐
- Customer Service ☐
- Decision-Making ☐
- Entrepreneurship ☐
- Group Processes ☐
- Influencing Skills ☐
- Innovation & Creativity ☐
- Interpersonal Relationships ☐
- Leadership ☐
- Creating a Learning Culture ☐
- Marketing, Sales and BD ☐
- Media Relations ☐
- Motivation ☐
- Negotiation Skills ☐
- Performance Management ☐
- Power Management Skills ☐
- Problem-Solving ☐
- Stakeholder Engagement ☐
- Strategy/Strategic Thinking ☐
- Strategic Business Growth ☐
- Stress Management ☐
- Supervisory Skills ☐
- Systems Thinking ☐
- Team Building/Teamwork ☐
- Time Management & Prioritisation ☐
- Transformational Leadership ☐

Thinking back over the last 12-18 months:
- What training worked, and why?

- What training did not work, and why?

How many people do you plan to have attending the program? _____

Over how many consecutive days are you planning for the training? _____

Would you like to consider an option of post-training coaching? _____

Executive Wisdom Consulting Group Pty Ltd
Willbert House, 68 Mayfield Road, Carina
QLD Australia 4152   ABN 64 011 012 758

Callback Request SMS: +61 412 728 113
info@executivewisdom.com
www.executivewisdom.com

EVALUATION TEMPLATE

Seven Steps to 360-Degree Success

Feedback evaluations are nearly always poorly completed because most are facilitated by people who just buy an off-the-shelf product thinking that one size fits all. Here's the rule: **You don't begin with questions**. You start with what information you're seeking to learn and validate, and then you back into the questions. The information you seek has to be tangible and verifiable for it to be worthwhile and for it to be evaluated.

For example, "increasing self-awareness and effectiveness" are not clear objectives for behaviour change. How will you know when she is more aware or more effective? The objectives must be clear, and only then do you work backwards and develop questions. Another example: The objective is to help the client become a better leader, which would include better delegation and development of subordinates. Questions might include: "What does Mary do that encourages or discourages subordinate development?" "When delegating, what would you say Mary does to support or frustrate those she has delegated to?"

The purpose of a 360 is to support personal development goals. Even before executing a 360, there are certain business goals to be achieved. Presumably, it has been determined that certain behaviours or skills are needed to satisfy the role of the job or move to the next level. 360 is to elicit evidence and to identify the specific leverage points needed to help this person grow and develop. If you use a scale of 1 - 10 (I prefer 1 - 5), it must be evident what each number means or you risk getting invalid answers. One person will give an 8 because Mary is better than everyone else and another will give a 6 because Mary isn't quite as good as she should be. You need to explicitly state what 1 means, 10, and everything in between. My personal preference is to do 360's in person, interviewing the people one by one. But if that is not possible, by telephone. So, my seven steps are:

1. Find the critical components of the job, not generalities (e.g. "lead meetings").
2. Design the questions to elicit evidence of behaviour, i.e. What information am I trying to get?
3. Choose the appropriate people to interview (e.g. position, tenure, etc.).
4. Be prepared to ask follow-up questions.
5. Look for patterns.
6. Report findings, not solutions.
7. Agree on the next steps.

Bring the best executive management learning to your organisation by having the 4-Day MBA delivered in-house. Contact us to arrange a telephone appointment to discuss your options for the development of your management team. E-mail: ric@mba4day.com or send a SMS to: +61 412 728 113 for a callback.

MANAGEMENT RESOURCES GUIDE

STRATEGY GUIDE

Cirque du Soleil — Developing a Blue Ocean Strategy

Notwithstanding a long-term decline in the circus industry, Cirque du Soleil profitably increased revenue 22-fold over 10 years by reinventing the service. Rather than competing within the confines of the existing industry or trying to take customers away from competitors, Cirque established uncontested market space that made the competition irrelevant. Cirque developed a blue ocean, a previously unknown market space. In blue oceans, demand is created rather than fought over. There is ample opportunity for growth that is both profitable and rapid. In red oceans—that is, all the industries already existing—companies compete by fighting for a greater share of limited demand. As the market space becomes more crowded, prospects for profits and growth decline. Products turn into commodities, and increasing competition turns the water bloody.

There are two ways to create blue oceans.

1. Launch completely new industries, as eBay did with online auctions.
2. Develop a blue ocean from within a red ocean by expanding the boundaries of an existing industry.

In studying more than 150 blue ocean creations in over 30 industries the authors of Blue Ocean Strategy observed that the traditional units of strategic analysis—company and industry—are of limited use in explaining how and why blue oceans are created. The most appropriate unit of analysis is the strategic move, the set of managerial actions and decisions involved in making a major market-creating business offering. Creating blue oceans builds brands. So powerful is blue ocean strategy, in fact, that a blue ocean strategic move can create brand equity that lasts for decades.

DISCUSSION QUESTIONS

- Are there companies in your industry that have created blue oceans?
- To what extent does your company's strategy rely on competing in existing market spaces?
- Do you have the right balance between line extensions and new initiatives?
- Do you rely too much on technology to open up new market opportunities?
- What initiatives have successfully broken the value/cost trade-off?
- What is preventing your company from creating a blue ocean?
- Are there obstacles you need to overcome?

Need a professional to facilitate your organisation's strategic planning? E-mail: ric@mba4day.com

HOW TO ENGAGE RIC WILLMOT & EXECUTIVE WISDOM

Ric Willmot believes that the best way to communicate is to speak directly with the people making the decisions. To that end, complete the form below and e-mail it to ric@executivewisdom.com or send it as a text message to +61 412.728-113 and Ric will telephone you within 24 hours.

Expression of Interest

Type of professional service required? ☑

- ◈ In-House Training ❑
- ◈ Coaching & Mentoring ❑
- ◈ Organisational Development Program ❑
- ◈ Professional Speaking ❑
- ◈ Consulting ❑
- ◈ Board Member ❑

When do you plan for this to commence (date)? _____

Your name: _____

Your position: _____

Organisation: _____

Address: _____
_____

Contact telephone and email (please print clearly): _____
_____

What is the best time to telephone you? _____

Send this completed form by email to ric@executivewisdom.com or take a photo with your smartphone and text message it to **+61 412.728-113** and Ric Willmot will telephone you personally within 24 hours.

www.ingramcontent.com/pod-product-compliance
Lightning Source LLC
Chambersburg PA
CBHW082338220526
45470CB00008B/2555